CREATE

your own

ONLINE STORE

{ *using* WORDPRESS }

IN A WEEKEND

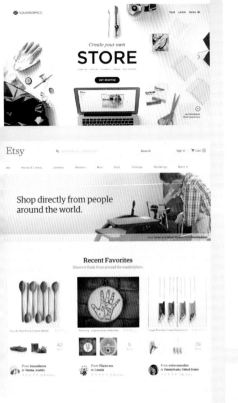
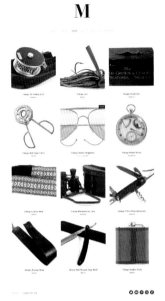

CREATE

your own

ONLINE
STORE

{ *using* **WORDPRESS** }

IN A WEEKEND

ALANNAH MOORE

ilex

CREATE YOUR OWN ONLINE STORE {USING WORDPRESS} IN A WEEKEND

First published in the United Kingdom in 2014 by
ILEX
210 High Street
Lewes
East Sussex
BN7 2NS

Distributed worldwide (except North America) by Thames & Hudson Ltd., 181A High Holborn, London WC1V 7QX, United Kingdom

Copyright © 2014 The Ilex Press Limited

Publisher: Alastair Campbell
Creative Director: James Hollywell
Executive Publisher: Roly Allen
Managing Editor: Nick Jones
Senior Project Editor: Natalia Price-Cabrera
Specialist Editor: Frank Gallaugher
Project Editor: Ellie Wilson
Commissioning Editor: Zara Larcombe
Editorial Assistant: Rachel Silverlight
Art Director: Julie Weir
Design: Simon Goggin

British Library Cataloguing-in-Publication Data
A catalogue record for this book is available from the British Library.

ISBN: 978 1 78157 143 9

Colour Origination by Ivy Press Reprographics

Printed and bound in China

CONTENTS

INTRODUCTION

The internet has changed the way we shop beyond all recognition. Global e-commerce sales reached $1.25 trillion in 2013 and, of course, the indications are that this will only increase.

The advantages for the shopper are clear. It's a timesaver and it's often more convenient—there's no need to leave home, and shopping can even be done on the move with a smartphone (not surprisingly this is a habit that's growing among shoppers). In addition, it's often cheaper to shop online and you can compare prices easily; the choice is far wider, and you can purchase pretty much anything.

But for the business owner, as well, the attraction of selling online is great. You can access a global market, or at least as wide a market as you are prepared to ship to. Your overheads are less, and you can be "open" 24 hours a day, every day of the week.

Most importantly, the internet offers a level playing field. If you have a professional-looking website and products that people want to buy, you stand as much of a chance of making your online business a success as the next person, even if that person has considerably more money to invest.

The great news for the small business person or entrepreneur is that while setting up a full-blown, made-from-scratch e-commerce website is an expensive, time-consuming, and complicated undertaking, there are an increasing number of solutions that put the creation of an online sales system well within anyone's reach, and many of these can be achieved relatively quickly.

There are solutions for everyone, some more expensive, some slightly more technical, some requiring more time invested to complete the setup. Whether you're selling your own products or someone else's, whether you're selling services online or downloadable files, there will be an e-commerce solution that's just right for you—within your financial reach, within your capabilities, and which won't need months of planning to achieve.

What this book will do for you

In this book we'll look at some of the fast and simple systems now available to the online entrepreneur. Multiple systems exist, and it can be hard work to figure out which will be easy to implement, against those which will cause the non-programmer a headache to set up and work with, and those which will need expensive and unexpected add-ons in order to do the job.

For this book, I've selected the options I think are the best choices, based on these criteria:

> **The system can be set up quickly and painlessly, without you having to hire a web developer.**
> **It is, of course, secure.**
> **It looks excellent.**

So that you can choose which one will work best for you, we'll analyze which systems require more technical expertise, which cost more, and which are best suited to particular kinds of business. For each system, we'll attempt to balance out the pros and cons so you can make an informed decision, and then guide you through the steps to implement the solution you decide upon.

We'll look at the different ways of taking payment via the internet and see which will be the most appropriate for you. We'll show you how you can present your products to maximum advantage, including marketing your store, social media, and how best to prepare your site for the search engines. Later in the book, we'll equip you with the knowledge you need to manage and develop your rapidly growing online business, and see some of the different ways webstore owners can increase their sales.

Within just days, you'll have your own online store and be taking payments online—you'll be a part of the online sales revolution.

COMPANION WEBSITE
The companion website to this book is www.createyouronlinestoreinaweekend.com. Check for updates, live examples, and interviews with successful online store owners.

2. A WEBSTORE

A webstore is an all-in-one system that comprises the site design with hosting and a built-in shopping cart. You need to input your payment details (more about this in Chapter 3) and your site content, product info, and so on, and you're ready to go.

The advantages of this kind of system are that you have a choice of great-looking templates that you can modify, you don't have to worry about technicalities or security, and the system is very easy to use. Additionally, a host of add-ons make it easy to integrate your all-in-one webstore with other needs such as mailing list systems and inventory control. Obviously, there are costs associated with such a service that make it more expensive to run a webstore than to sell via Amazon or eBay, or to do the whole thing yourself using the WordPress system.

TERMINOLOGY

Like "storefront," the term "webstore" is often used to refer to any kind of online shop; here we'll use it to refer to an all-in-one system, to make a clear distinction between the two.

Setting up your store via a webstore provider gives you your own online presence. It's quick and easy to set up and removes the hassle of hosting your own site. Above: www.cookbookvillage.com set up with Shopify.

3. WORDPRESS

WordPress is a free software system that you can use to run an online store on your own web host.

This is a great solution if you want your own store but you don't have the budget for an all-in-one webstore system with its monthly payments. While the setup is not too technical, it is not as straightforward as using a webstore system and does require a certain amount of application.

Wonderful-looking professional templates will make your site look as good as it would using an all-in-one webstore system, and an added plus is knowing you're in charge of your own site, rather than being dependent on an external company.

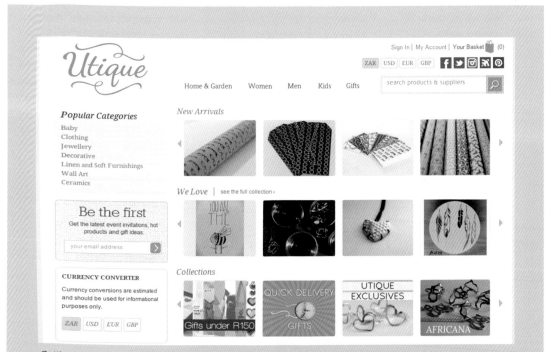

Setting up your site via WordPress is a little trickier to navigate, but your online store will be entirely your own, and you'll avoid the monthly fees of a webstore provider. Above: www.utique.co.za.

Squarespace (www.squarespace.com)

Until recently, Squarespace was mainly used for blogs and online creative portfolios, but now it offers e-commerce, which makes it a great option if you want a visually focused, ultra-slick, "designer" appearance for your store. At the time of writing, Squarespace is currently only available if you're in the U.S., Canada, and the UK. Payments are accepted via Stripe, with no other option available.

Marquee template

Montauk template

Adironack template

Aviator template

Weebly (www.weebly.com)

An extremely user-friendly interface means creating a website is really easy and very affordable (free if you don't mind a Weebly link and you can even get e-commerce with the basic, free setup); the tradeoff is that while there is a large selection, the templates aren't as stunning-looking as they might be.

Webs (www.webs.com)

Webs has been around for more than ten years and is a hugely popular all-in-one website builder. Like Weebly, the Webs interface is amazingly easy to use. You can sell online even with the free version, though you're limited to five items (also note that the free version doesn't offer support). A downside is that there aren't many templates to choose from, but there is a good variety of apps, including a social media toolbar, Etsy shop, appointment-booker, and website chat.

Jimdo (www.jimdo.com)

Another user-friendly store builder (though not drag-and-drop), Jimdo runs in twelve different languages and offers good back-end store admin facilities (even available with the free version, although, as with Weebly, you're limited to five items). Their support forum is impressive, but the designs aren't the slickest. They have recently extended their range of templates though, for example to allow full-screen video backgrounds.

Moonfruit (www.moonfruit.com)

An easy-to-use, UK-based system that allows you to create a great-looking site and sell products from it within minutes. While the e-commerce management side of things is rather basic, and the store system only accepts PayPal, the templates look great—they are among the best around—and you can easily integrate your shop into Facebook. The free version allows you to set up a shop selling unlimited products, but the Moonfruit branding will be visible, as shown in the screenshots; at the time of writing, a blog feature for the latest version was under development.

High Spec theme   Urban Life theme   Mochi theme

Create (www.create.net)

Another UK-based webstore system with an impressive feature list and an easy-to-use interface. Favored by the craft community, Create accepts a range of payment gateways and caters to users worldwide.

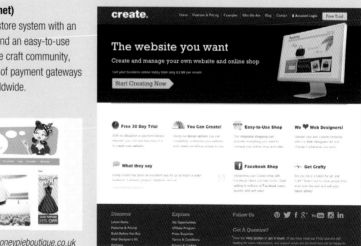

Honeypie Boutique: www.honeypieboutique.co.uk

How to choose a DOMAIN NAME

In order to get up and running, you will need to decide on and purchase a domain name for your new webstore. (Your domain name is your address on the web, something like www.yourstore.com.)

Most webstore systems will allow you to run your store with the initial address they give you (for example, www.mystore.mybigcommerce.com), but in order to look like a professional business, you really need to purchase your own domain name. (Note that with the vast majority of storefronts, you don't get the option of using your own domain.)

Your domain name could be:
> **your brand name or business name**
> **a name composed of search engine keywords (such as the kind of products you sell)**
> **something creative that's altogether different (see "Ideas for domain names")**

When choosing a domain name, make sure you don't choose anything that's too similar to your competition. Do also check your chosen name doesn't resemble anyone else's trademark.

Ideas for domain names
Many .com domain names have already been registered. Here are some ideas to help you find something available or come up with something new.
> Use a phrase or slogan.
> Use a deliberate misspelling
> Invent a name.
> Combine words.
> Use words from different languages.
> Use your brand or business name and add "store," "web," or something else on to the end.
> Make use of one of the many online tools that can help you come up with something unique (see the box below).

Online tools to help you come up with a name
> www.dotomator.com
> namestation.com
> www.nameboy.com
> www.domainsbot.com
> www.randomainer.com
> impossibility.org
> domai.nr (getting creative with unusual and country-specific extensions)

CHOOSING AN EXTENSION

The extension (also known as "TLD," top level domain) is the part of the domain name after the dot, i.e. the "com" or the "co.uk" part.

In most cases, it's advisable to choose a .com domain, as it looks most professional, and can be remembered easily.

However, choosing a country-specific extension such as .co.uk, .fr, .es, and so on, may suit you better if you don't want to do business globally, for example if shipping costs make this prohibitive.

REGISTERING YOUR DOMAIN NAME

For many, the easiest option will be to register your domain name via your webstore provider. However, if you're not certain whether you will remain with the same system indefinitely, it makes sense to register it independently with a registrar.

Two reliable domain name registrars are:

Godaddy
(www.godaddy.com)
Namecheap
(www.namecheap.com)

For international registrations, look at:

Gandi
(www.gandi.net)
101 Domain
(www.101domain.com)
Macaria
(www.marcaria.com).

Do compare prices for international registrations, as these can vary significantly.

If you register your domain with an independent registrar, you'll need to change the nameserver settings from within the management area of your registrar's website. This will connect your domain name to your new webstore. Look for "DNS" or "Domain Name Server Setup" from within the admin area; your webstore provider will give you the correct nameserver information to paste into the fields in this area. You may find it takes several hours for your nameservers to switch over.

TIP

Researching domain names
Googling a domain name isn't a sure-fire way to see if it is available. The owner may simply not be using it. Instead, search for it via a registrar's website, such as Godaddy. To find out who the owner is of an already-registered domain name, try betterwhois.com.

Website hosting FOR WORDPRESS

Website hosting is the space you rent in cyberspace to house your new website. For the webstore and storefront systems looked at in this book, you will not need to take out your own website hosting, as this will be included in your package. But if you are going for the WordPress option, you will need to get set up with a web host in order to set up your webstore.

HOW TO CHOOSE A WEB HOST

There are hundreds of web hosting companies to choose from and it's essential that yours is reliable—you don't want to find your website is "unavailable" to potential customers.

As far as technicalities go, in order to set up WordPress, you need to choose a hosting package capable of running PHP and MySQL. You will almost certainly also want to choose a company that features a "one-click" WordPress install, as this will make your setup infinitely easier than installing WordPress manually. (You may see this feature mentioned by name as "Fantastico," "Simple Scripts," or "Installatron"— whichever system your web host uses is absolutely fine.)

You'll most likely be able to see the web host's "uptime" record posted on its website— if you can see that it is "up" (i.e. running correctly) 99 or 100% of the time, you can be assured its service is reliable. It must also offer 24/7 technical support so that if you ever run into any difficulties, you can be certain of a prompt response.

In addition, you may want to choose a hosting package that offers unlimited storage—so that you don't have to worry about the number of products you showcase or the number of images of them you upload to the site—and unlimited bandwidth, to be sure you can cope with the impact of a flood of traffic to your site. Unlimited email addresses is also a good idea, so if you need to, you can set up different email addresses for sales, enquiries, after sales, press, and so on.

Recommended hosts that offer all the above criteria are:

Bluehost
(www.bluehost.com)
Dreamhost
(www.dreamhost.com)

You will find others that fulfil your criteria, and the choice is entirely yours. However, if your language is not English, you will probably want to set up with a local host that offers you the features discussed above, so that you can access support in your own language.

SHARED OR VIRTUAL PRIVATE SERVER (VPS)?

A "shared" hosting package will usually be adequate for the needs of a small- to medium-sized webstore, but if in doubt, ask the hosting company.

SHOPPING CART SOFTWARE

There are excellent, multi-featured "open source" shopping cart softwares (meaning they are free and available to everyone) that you can use if you have your own web host setup. The best are Zen Cart, OsCommerce, and PrestaShop. We are not focusing on these in the book as to use them the average person would need some technical knowledge or professional help, but if you do have some technical skill, you may find one of these systems suits your needs perfectly.

Bluehost is a reputable host perfect for a WordPress installation. Above: www.bluehost.com

Registering your name through your hosting company

Most web hosts will include a domain name with your package. This is an easy option to go for, in that you will be dealing with one company rather than two. However, if you anticipate changing your web host at any time in the future, or using an all-in-one webstore later down the line, registering your domain name with an independent registrar may make your life easier later on.

While it's fine to register your domain name with your hosting company, it is not advisable to take out web hosting with a domain name registrar, although it's likely they will offer it to you—a dedicated hosting company will usually meet your hosting requirements better.

SSL

SSL stands for "Secure Sockets Layer" and is a system used to encrypt sensitive information input via your website, such as your customers' credit card numbers and other personal data, helping to keep it safe from hackers.

It isn't always necessary to have your website protected by SSL. For example, if your customers are submitting a payment to you via PayPal, if they type their information directly into the PayPal interface, they are protected by PayPal's SSL. But with many webstore systems, your customers will be typing their information into your shopping cart interface, so even if you are using PayPal to accept their payment, you do need SSL to make sure they are protected.

Some webstore systems include an SSL certificate, but some require you to purchase one independently. This will vary from system to system, so consult the comparison table on pages 16–19 for information, or ask the webstore provider for more precise details.

It's a fact that customers are often reassured by seeing the "https://" at the beginning of your website address; it shows that SSL is in place on the website, so any transactions that occur will do so in a secure environment. This may be enough of a reason to purchase an SSL certificate, even when it isn't strictly necessary. This won't be a concern if you're operating a storefront as your payments will be processed by Amazon or eBay and therefore protected by Amazon or eBay's security system.

As soon as we log into Amazon.com, the padlock and the "https://" in the address bar shows us our details are secure.

3

Taking payment online

IN ORDER TO COLLECT PAYMENT FROM YOUR
CUSTOMERS VIA YOUR ONLINE STORE, YOU NEED
TO HAVE A PAYMENT SYSTEM SET UP.

PayPal

PayPal is king when it comes to taking money quickly and easily online. Most of the systems talked about in this book offer PayPal as a payment processor, and for some (though not the ones we focus on in detail), it's the only way that you can take payments from your customers. Amazon is an exception, in that they pay you directly into your bank account; Squarespace (see page 26) only works with Stripe. Some of the stores that allow you to sell your designs online (see pages 21–28) may pay you directly, but for the most part, PayPal is the obvious, and in some cases the only, option.

If you don't have an account, it's simple to set one up at www.paypal.com. In order to accept credit or debit card payments (rather than just having your customers pay you from their PayPal account, which is limiting if it's the only option), you need to sign up for, or upgrade to, a Premier or Business account. The main difference between a Premier and Business account is that you can't use your business name with a Premier account.

For your account to be functional, PayPal needs first to verify your bank account, which can be done quickly via online banking. PayPal will transfer a small amount of money to your account with a number as a reference; you then type this into your PayPal account. For a Business account, however, PayPal will need to give you approval, which can take several days. To set up a Business account, you need to have your business information to hand, including your business bank account details and your business address (the precise details required will vary from country to country). If you don't have all this ready yet, or you're in a hurry to start taking payment from your site, you can sign up for a Premier account, get your bank account verified, and upgrade to a Business account at a later date. To sign up for a Premier account, you need to register for a Personal account, and you'll then be asked if you want a Premier account during the signup process.

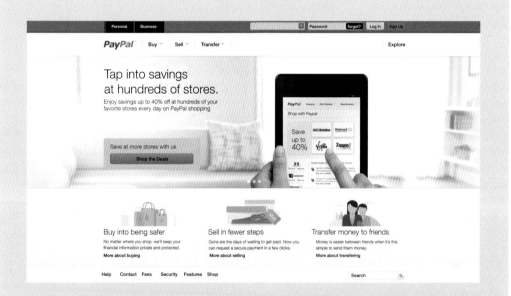

ACCEPTING PAYMENTS WITH PAYPAL VIA YOUR WEBSTORE

With some webstore systems you have a choice of PayPal payment solutions, although these will vary depending on where you are based. The most commonly used option (and the only one, with many systems) is PayPal Payments Standard. Here, the customer is taken to the PayPal site to make their payment, then transferred back to your webstore afterward. Some webstore systems may offer you other options: PayPal Payments Advanced, for which there is a monthly fee, allows the customers to check out on your site without transferring to PayPal; PayPal Payments Pro, with a higher monthly fee, also allows you to accept credit cards by phone or mail. PayPal Express Checkout is an additional option for you to offer your customers if you're using an alternative payment gateway, so that they can pay quickly and easily by PayPal if they choose to.

4

The look of the site
THE IMAGE YOU PRESENT TO THE WORLD.

Conveying the RIGHT IMAGE

The way your website looks is essential. It's the only chance you get to present your business to the world. Unlike with a brick-and-mortar store, you won't get a chance to engage your customers in conversation to help them decide to buy; if the first sight of your webstore fails to engage with your customers, they will click away.

With a storefront on a big marketplace, you won't be able to customize your site to a large degree, but you can make sure you have a good logo to reinforce your branding and look as professional as possible.

One advantage of a webstore, over a site built from scratch, is that you'll be starting from a beautiful and polished template, which you'll then customize. There's no

doubt that your site will look professional, and essential aspects such as clarity of layout and usability, which are major factors to consider, will already have been covered.

However, what you do need to invest serious thought into is the right "look and feel" for your customers. Think about who you are selling to. What kind of look and feel would your prospective customers want? What kind of image do you want to create of your business? Does your site need to look commercial and well-established, or should it look more personal and quirky? Should it look modern, or traditional? Are your customers conservative, or cutting-edge? Your site needs to resonate with your customers from the get-go, so spend time imagining how they'd like your site to look.

There are dozens of templates to choose from, to suit all kinds of businesses. It's essential the style you choose engages your prospective customers. Top: Bedazzled (Bigcommerce), Classic (Bigcommerce); middle: Dooley, Wood (Shopify), Editions, Dark (Shopify); below: Knack (Volusion), Limitless, Restore (Shopify).

Your LOGO

Your online business needs to have an effective logo. A logo performs some essential functions. First off, it makes your site memorable and distinguishes your business from the other webstores, perhaps selling similar products, that your potential customers will almost certainly also visit. It needs to be correctly pitched and fit the image you want to display, so that straightaway it will resonate with your customers and they'll be more easily persuaded you're the company they want to do business with. A great-looking logo will also make you look professional from the moment they click onto your site, and this is the first step to creating trust with your customers.

Since it's so important, you may want to get a logo designed professionally. There are a number of online services that can do this for you—see the box below right.

A logo makes your site look professional, as well as creating a memorable visual reminder for your potential customers. From top: www.littlejoydesigns.co.uk, www.happypuzzle.co.uk, www.uppercasemagazine.com (logo by Janine Vangool).

TIP

Transparent backgrounds
You'll need your logo on a transparent background so that you can use it on your site, no matter what color is behind it.

Places to get a logo made

> Crowd Spring (www.crowdspring.com)
> Design Crowd (www.designcrowd.com)
> 99 Designs (99designs.com)
> Elance (www.elance.com)

Alternatively, an easy and effective way to create a logo yourself is simply to choose a distinctive font that suits the image of your business, and create a "logo" by writing your business or store name in this font. Any graphics software, such as Photoshop, Photoshop Elements, or Gimp, will enable you to do this, or you can simply use the free online service Pixlr. com (as shown on the following page). Try www.1001freefonts. com for interesting fonts you can download to your computer. It's for both Mac and PC, and downloading and installing a font to your computer will also make it accessible in Pixlr. Since you're using the font for commercial use, you'll need to upgrade to their paid-for commercial package, but the price is extremely reasonable.

REINFORCING YOUR BRAND

Once you have your logo you'll want to use it on your stationery— letterheads, bills, wrapping materials, etc. Postcards, stickers, and printed labels are also good ways of reinforcing your branding. Have a look at Moo.com for ideas. Other ways to echo your website branding are to use your website accent colors on labels or packaging, or carry the fonts used on the site through to any other printed material—price lists, compliment slips, and the like.

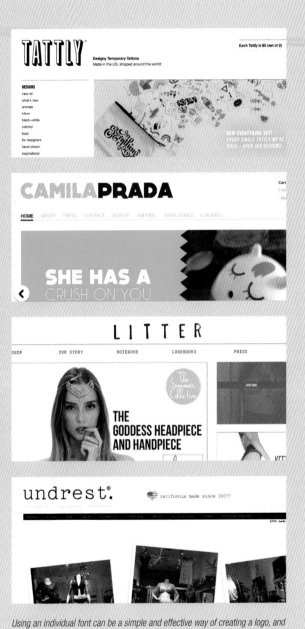

Using an individual font can be a simple and effective way of creating a logo, and is a great solution if you haven't budgeted for something professionally designed. From top: tattly.com, camilaprada.com, littersf.com, undrest.com

Creating a title "logo" for your site
USING PIXLR.COM

If you don't have any specialized graphics software on your computer, you can use Pixlr.com, a free online graphics program, to create a title "logo" for your site. Here's how to do it.

1. Go to www.pixlr.com and click "Pixlr Advanced."

2. Select "Create a new image."

3. Type a title for the file in the Name field. Your webstore system may specify the dimensions for your logo file; if so, type the pixel dimensions in the Width and Height boxes. (Pixels are the unit of measurement used for images on websites. If the size is written as "250 x 100," the first number is the width, the second the height.) If no dimensions are specified, leave the dimensions as they are as you will be able to crop the image before you save it. Check the box next to "Transparent" as this will mean you can use your logo no matter what color the background is on your website. Click "OK."

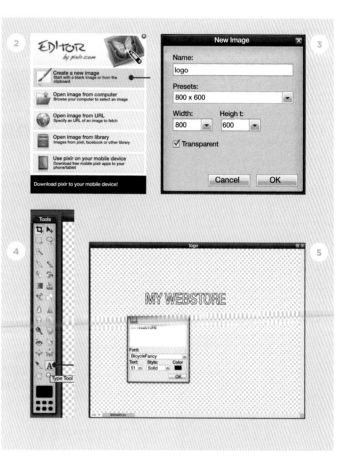

4. From the toolbar on the left of your screen, select the Type tool, which is shown as an "A."

5. Click anywhere inside your file (the gray and white checked area) and type your webstore or business name in the text box. Choose the font, size, style, and color, and click "OK." (Do not be surprised that the background is showing as checked gray and white squares—this simply means that the background is transparent. It will not show up like this on your website.)

6. Select the Crop tool from the left-hand toolbar, which is the item at the top left. (If you already specified the dimensions of your file, you can skip to step 8.)

7. Use the tool to draw a box with your mouse, as closely around the lettering as you can without touching it. Select the Crop tool again, and then when asked if you want to apply the changes, click "Yes."

8. Now choose File > Save from the Pixlr menu as shown (not from your browser menu!).

9. In the window that opens, choose "PNG" from the drop-down labeled Format (this keeps your background transparent), slide the slider labeled Quality right up to 100%, and click "OK."

10. Choose where you want to save the image on your computer, click "Save," and you're done. When you're ready, you'll be able to upload your new logo to your website.

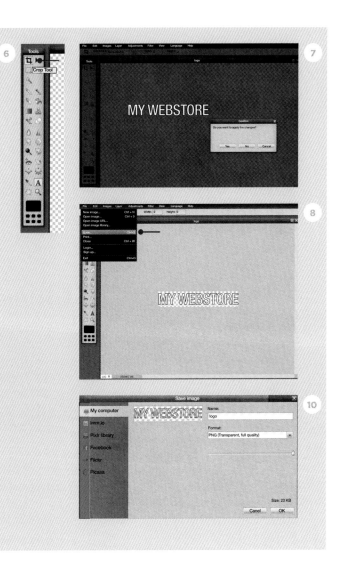

5

The content of the site
THE ACTUAL CONTENT OF YOUR SITE
AND WHERE TO PUT IT.

The pages YOU NEED

THE HOME PAGE

The home page is the first page that your customers see, so it has to engage them immediately. Your layout may depend on the template you choose, but here are some points to consider.

First off, you want to show your visitors straightaway that you can provide what they are looking for. So, you'll want to display your bestselling products, or at least have very visible links to them. A "slider" or "carousel"—that is, a large enclosed area toward the top of the page that rotates, either automatically or when an arrow is clicked—is a common way of displaying important content in the most prominent position on the home page. You can put special offers, seasonal products, new products, or your bestsellers here, where you're sure people will see them. Be aware that the text you put on your home page is of great importance to the search engines. It's easy to find that your home page is mostly images—pictures of bestsellers, new products, etc.—but make sure you have text, including your main search terms, as well. (We'll look more thoroughly at search engines in Chapter 11.)

In addition, think about your USP—your "unique selling point." If your products are the best, or the cheapest, or you have the best deals, point this out very obviously. If you have a special deal, such as free delivery, write this on the home page.

A slider (or carousel) with rotating content is a great way of displaying important information to make sure no-one misses it. From above: www.giftlab.com, www. shoplatitude.com, www.elvafields.com

TIP

Getting creative with your slider images

Notice as you browse other online stores on the web how they have composed each of the images that make up their slider sequence. Each usually includes explanatory text as part of the image—as you can see on the websites shown on this page—with a call to action such as "Shop Now" to encourage the visitor to click on the image and be drawn further into the store. You can also combine several elements within one slider image.

OTHER PAGES

As well as the pages that describe your products, you'll want to include the following pages on your site:

> About—your chance to make the business come to life for your potential customers. If you can engage them, you stand a chance of converting them into buyers.
> Contact—include a telephone number, if possible, and a street address to show you're a bona fide business.
> Shipping/Delivery—say which countries you ship to, what the costs are, and how long delivery is expected to take.
> Return policy—state the time limit for returning unwanted goods, and whether return shipping is free.

> Terms & conditions—these need to be published on your site, and some systems will oblige your customers to check a checkbox to say they agree with them before they order (see Chapter 15).
> Privacy policy—this is a legal requirement (as above, see Chapter 15).
> Cookies—a cookie declaration is a requirement for websites based in the EU (again, see Chapter 15).
> Frequently Asked Questions (FAQ)/Help—this is a chance to answer any questions your customers have that may prevent them from buying.
> Press—show existing coverage, give links to online coverage, and give the contact details of the person who will deal with press enquiries.

Your About page is the place to let your customers know more about you, your vision, and the business. Here, a photograph of the founders and an introductory video make sure the visitor is fully engaged. Above: www.brika.com

Other elements you may want to include

> A search box so customers can find what they're looking for easily within your store.
> An email mailing list signup form—we'll talk more about email lists in Chapter 13.
> Social media badges and "share/follow" buttons—we'll go into detail about social media (Facebook, Twitter, and the like) in Chapter 12.
> Reviews
> Testimonials
> A blog—we'll see more about blogs in Chapter 10.

Your Contact page needs to show your street address and give a telephone number where you can be reached in case of queries. Above: www.torieandhoward.com

Writing your TEXT

When you're putting together the text for your store, there are certain aspects of writing for the web that you should bear in mind in order to make your text as effective as possible. Creating text for a website isn't at all the same as creating text for a printed document.

First off, when reading a website, people want the information they're looking for right away. Their attention spans are shorter when reading onscreen, perhaps because of the huge amount of information readily available to them. So, say what you need to say as clearly as possible, and don't be too wordy. If you have a lot of information you need to include, you don't have to cut it short, just break it up into easily digestible paragraphs and use plenty of visual signposts —headings, subheadings, and bullet points.

Make sure you leave plenty of blank space to give the eyes a break, and be sure your most important points are visible right away. These should be at the top of the page, in bold or in a larger heading style, and not hidden deep within paragraphs of text far down the page.

Another aspect to consider is making your copy customer-centric. Rather than telling visitors how great your business is, focus on how your products will help your customer. Think of benefits for the customer, not features, as you create your page text and your product descriptions. (There are some great examples over the page.)

Remember to keep your copy lively. You may have dozens of pages to create text for, and this may seem daunting, but keep it interesting! Your aim is to keep the customers on the page long enough to inspire them to buy from you—they'll quickly click away if your copy sounds tired or boring.

Your website text should also include specific calls to action. Make use of direct requests to "click here," "order now," or "buy" to inspire your visitors to make that crucial step.

Also think about the style of your writing. Whether it is formal or less formal will depend on your target market, but remember that you can also sound fun and interesting, at the same time as professional.

Finally, but crucially, when crafting your page text, think in terms of the search engines. You are writing for the search engines as well as for your customers. Your headings should include major search terms, and your product descriptions should be rich in keywords. We will look at search engines in more detail in Chapter 11; it's a good idea to read and absorb the information in that chapter before you start writing your website text.

TIP

Pay attention to your text
Double-check for typos and grammar mistakes. It's very easy to overlook these in copy you've written yourself, so if possible, ask someone else with a good eye for detail to look for mistakes for you. It's very important for your website visitors to see that your site looks professional, and a silly spelling mistake may undermine their trust in you; if your site looks sloppy, how can they trust you with their credit card details, and to deliver their purchases on time?

"A must-have for lovers of coziness, the lightweight material of this slouchy pullover makes this SWL original a perfect candidate for layering flannels, lace, and collars beneath it. Wearing our diamond heart will remind you that you are worth love and to be comfortable in your own skin and to step out fearlessly into the world. You might stumble, you might sway, but we promise we'll always stay close to your side."

* *Recognized as one of the best products of 2011 in a leading consumer research magazine*
* *Removable filter basket lifts out for fast and easy filling and cleaning*
* *Brewing pause 'n serve lets you pour a cup of coffee while the coffeemaker is still brewing*
* *Special cleaning cycle makes cleaning our coffeemaker quick and easy*
* *2-hour auto shut-off keeps your coffee hot for 2 hours, then automatically shuts off*

Different writing styles are appropriate for different types of website. Note that even though the Amazon text (right) is more formal, the copywriter has taken care to make the product text highlight the benefits of the product.
Above: www.soworthloving.com, above right: www.amazon.com

*"**Our Story:** Our town used to make 35,000 pairs of jeans every week for 40 years employing 400 people. Then in 2001 the factory closed. So we decided 4 decades worth of know-how shouldn't go to waste. That's why the Hiut Denim Company was born: To get the town making jeans again."*

The text of this webstore successfully engages the visitor by presenting the story of the products they are selling.
Above: hiutdenim.co.uk

Describing your products

There is some debate as to whether product descriptions are better long or short. In my opinion, longer is better for two reasons: first, you want to tell your customers everything they need to know in order to buy the product, and second, as long as all the content is relevant, longer descriptions are ideal material for the search engines. Just make sure you break up the text with line spaces, subheadings, and bullets, as mentioned, so your readers don't get lost while reading.

The following points are key when creating descriptions for your products:
> Make sure the product heading has the most important keywords in it, using a subheading if necessary for secondary keywords or phrases (see Chapter 11).
> Keep your product descriptions interesting.
> Give your customers all the information they need to know to buy. Don't leave them with any unanswered questions. This may be the difference between whether they buy from you, or from another competing website.

> Be sure to list all the features of your products, and wherever you can, present these as benefits to your customers, as shown in the example right.

In summary, think about your customers. What's in it for them to buy your product?

On your individual product pages, you should include:
> All information the customer may require, including features, dimensions, etc.
> Details of all possible variations—size, color, etc.
> Reviews, preferably independent ones. If your system doesn't allow you to include reviews, you can always include them in the product description text.
> Photos of different angles, details, etc. (see the next page).

"The original multi-award-winning ghd IV styler is the perfect tool for quick, effortless straightening and easy curls and waves. Advanced ceramic technology provides ultra fast heat up and heat recovery. A round barrel makes it easy to achieve beautiful waves and curls that last.

A handy sleep mode provides peace of mind and is activated if the styler isn't used for 30 minutes. Universal voltage ensures you'll get the same styling performance wherever you are in the world, making this styler a great choice if you travel frequently.

Suitable for all hair types and lengths. A brilliant all-rounder for everyday styling.

ghd authenticity guaranteed."

This is a brilliant example of product text that is interesting to read and entirely customer-centric. While all the features of the hair-styling tongs are clearly listed, each of them is presented as a benefit to the customer. Above: www.johnlewis.com/ghd-iv-hair-styler-mk4/p231760887

Photographing your PRODUCTS

The importance of good photography can't be overemphasized, bad photos can completely undermine the effect you've worked so hard to achieve. If at all possible, get your products photographed professionally, or ask your suppliers if they have good product photographs that you can use. However, bear in mind that all photographs you show on the site should be in the same style, so you won't want to use some provided by the supplier, as well as some you or someone else has taken.

If the cost of hiring a photographer is prohibitive, here are some tips for photographing your products yourself. Today's smartphone cameras are so sophisticated that if you don't have access to anything more fancy, you'll find that with a little care and by following the tips below, you can achieve results that are perfectly adequate.

Tips for photographing your products yourself

> Create a staging area in which to place the products. Consider the horizontal surface that the item will rest on, and the vertical area behind it. Alternatively, buy a roll of white paper and unroll it so that it provides a continuous backdrop and horizontal surface, thereby creating a completely white, professional looking background. Or buy a lightbox (also called a light tent)—these are very inexpensive, so if you have a large number of photographs to take for your site, it may be worth the investment.

> You may want to add other just-visible items to create an atmosphere (for example, other tableware items such as knife and fork, glass, napkin, if you are displaying a plate), but don't let these distract from the main item.

> Surround the item with multiple light sources, so there aren't any harsh shadows on one side of the object. A lightbox (light tent) is ideal as it diffuses the light, preventing any glare.

Holding a sheet of paper between the light and the item you're photographing is another way of reducing glare (don't tape the paper as it could be a fire risk—get someone to hold it for you).

> Make sure you zoom in on the product (or crop it afterwards)—you don't want too much extra space around it.

> Eliminate camera shake and create a consistent angle for your photos by propping your camera on a level surface, or by using a tripod.

> Take care to make your lighting consistent by using similar lighting conditions for each series of shots.

> Make use of the Macro mode, if your camera has this option, to shoot details. This will mean your main subject is in focus, but the background is not, and the photo will have a professional look.

PREPARING YOUR IMAGES FOR THE WEB

Use a graphics software such as Photoshop Elements, Gimp, or Pixlr.com to crop your photos and resize them to the exact pixel dimension they need to be for your site. (Images for websites are measured in pixels, but your system may refer to the proportion that the images should be, instead of giving pixel dimensions.) Your webstore system might crop and resize your images automatically, but doing it yourself beforehand allows you total control over the way the images are cropped, and prevents any distortion.

You may find that there is a limit to the file size you can upload to your store. If this is the case, use software such as those mentioned above to reduce the size of the image.

Your photos should be saved as .jpg or .jpeg format.

TIP

Get ideas for product photos
Spend some time looking at other webstores, noting carefully the way in which their products are photographed. Is there an effect you particularly like? Can you achieve a similar effect?

Using the Crop tool in Pixlr, you can choose the "Aspect ratio" or "Output size" drop-down to resize your image.

When you save your file from Pixlr, you can reduce the file size, if necessary, using the Quality slider.

Building TRUST

Establishing trust with your website visitors is a big part of converting them into paying customers. When they arrive on your site they don't know you, and, unlike in a brick-and-mortar store, you can't chat with them to make them feel comfortable.

Your About page is a chance to present your business as one with real people behind it; we've also mentioned how you should give a telephone number on your Contact page if possible, and show your real-life street address.

Even after you've made a sale, take care to look after your customer. Build a relationship with them—if you cherish your customers, you stand a good chance of turning them into repeat customers.

The following measures will also help reinforce the feeling that your business is trustworthy:

> Offer a no-quibbles guarantee so that your visitors can feel confident enough to buy, and offer free shipping for returns, if this is viable.
> Be upfront about delivery charges.
> State clearly when something is out of stock. Customers hate to feel they may be tricked into making an order when something isn't actually available.
> Allow customers plenty of time to return goods.
> Keep the customer informed. Confirm dispatch, and, when possible, give tracking numbers.
> Display payment gateway badges when possible.
> Display any badges of groups and associations you belong to.
> Publish testimonials and reviews on your site.

Displaying payment gateway badges can help your customers feel secure.

Displaying delivery information clearly— charges, and the time it will take for the goods to reach the customer—helps your visitors believe your business is trustworthy. Right: www.lucylovesthis.com.

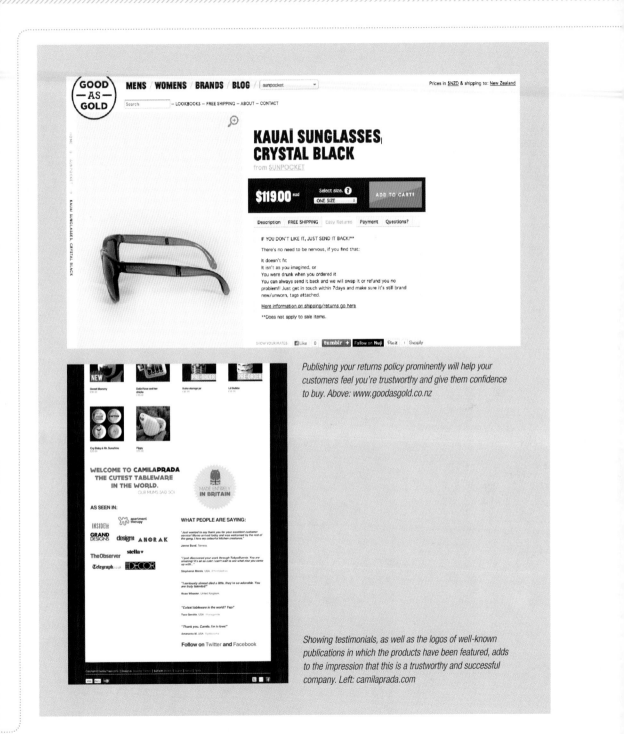

Publishing your returns policy prominently will help your customers feel you're trustworthy and give them confidence to buy. Above: www.goodasgold.co.nz

Showing testimonials, as well as the logos of well-known publications in which the products have been featured, adds to the impression that this is a trustworthy and successful company. Left: camilaprada.com

6

In focus: storefronts

SETTING UP A STOREFRONT WITHIN A WELL-KNOWN MARKETPLACE IS A VERY EASY WAY OF SELLING ONLINE, AND ONE THAT CAN BE VERY SUCCESSFUL.

An Amazon STOREFRONT

Setting up an Amazon storefront is one of the quickest ways of getting your products out there for sale; as soon as you sign up as a seller and start listing your products, you'll instantly have access to the millions of potential customers who use Amazon. Your products will show up when someone searches those products, whether or not they know of your existence or even visit your storefront where all your products are listed together. When you choose to list your products on Amazon, you avoid the costs of setting up your own online store, and while you don't get much of an opportunity to build your brand as the customization possibilities are very limited, your customers already know and trust Amazon, and you get to benefit from this before you've generated your first review, or even made a single sale.

With an Amazon storefront, your branding is reduced to a minimum, but your products will be available to millions. Big Box Bargains: http://www.amazon.com/shops/A2QTFB4KIJUXCQ.

Sign-up requirements

In order to sign up for an Amazon storefront you need to have a phone number where you can be reached, your tax information on hand, and an internationally chargeable credit card (so your fees can be deducted even if you don't make any sales).

To be paid, you need a bank account in the U.S., the UK, or the eurozone. You don't need to be based in the U.S. to sign up to sell on Amazon. com, but you do need to be able to ship to the U.S. (whether or not you use the Fulfillment by Amazon service), and to conduct all customer service in English.

Note that in order to list your products on Amazon you'll need a product code for each item (see the box on page 60), and you'll also need all product information handy (the manufacturer, dimensions, etc.), as well as clear product photographs taken against a white background, as per Amazon's guidelines.

SETTING UP YOUR AMAZON STOREFRONT

1. Go to www.amazon.com and click the link labeled "Sell" above the search box.

2. Choose whether you want a Professional or Individual account—see the box opposite; it's likely you'll need to choose a Professional account.

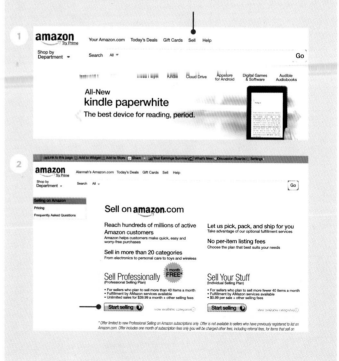

3. Follow the registration process; you can sign in with an existing Amazon account, or you can create a new account. During the process you'll receive an email welcoming you to Amazon Seller Central, but you won't actually be able to access this until you have completed the registration process. The process has five parts:

    i. Your Selling Plan—this is where you choose between an Individual or Professional account and whether you're going to use the Fulfillment by Amazon service (you'd come back here if you wanted to change your plan in the future).

    ii. Your Seller Information— your address.

    iii. Your Charge Method— your bank account information.

    iv. Your Identity Verification— you can choose to either receive a call or a text message giving you a PIN number that you input into the system to confirm verification.

    v. Your Tax Identity Information—this will be checked, but you can go on and set up your products once you've input your information.

AN "INDIVIDUAL" OR A "PROFESSIONAL" ACCOUNT?

There are certain categories of products you can't sell without a Professional account, including jewelry, collectibles, and car parts, for which you need to get approval. If you're unsure of which service you need to sign up for, go to this page: services.amazon.com/selling/benefits.htm, where there's a table comparing what you can and can't do with each. If you're planning to sell more than 40 items a month, you need a Professional account.

Fulfillment by Amazon (FBA)

One of the great benefits of listing on Amazon—apart from being able to access such a huge marketplace of customers ready to order—is the option to use Fulfillment by Amazon. This is a fabulous service that allows Amazon to handle all your order fulfillment for you, from storing your products to packing and shipping them, and even dealing with customer service. It works on a pay-as-you-go basis, so you're only charged for orders that are fulfilled, and your customers can benefit from free Super Saver Shipping and Amazon Prime at no extra cost to you. Plus, the "Fulfillment by Amazon" badge that will display next to your product listing helps build customers' confidence in buying from you. Note you can also use the FBA system for your dispatch, independently of an Amazon storefront.

4. Having completed your registration, you'll find yourself inside Seller Central. This is where you upload your product details (as well as access your orders, reports, feedback, etc.). Products can be added to Amazon's product catalog individually—you can either add a product that is already for sale by someone else on Amazon, or create an entirely new listing for the product if it isn't already in the Amazon catalog. Alternatively, you can upload product information via a spreadsheet created from a downloadable template that is specific to the type of products you're inputting.

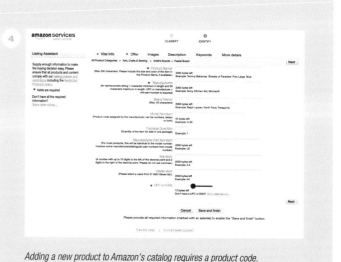

Adding a new product to Amazon's catalog requires a product code.

What Is an SKU?

An "SKU," or Stock-Keeping Unit, is the code or number assigned by a merchant to a particular product so that it can be tracked for inventory purposes. You'll need to assign different SKUs to every variation of a product, for example an item of clothing in a particular size will have one SKU, a different size will have a different SKU, the same size but a different color will have yet another SKU, and so on.

Product codes

A product code—UPC (Universal Product Code), EAN (European Article Number), JAN (Japanese Article Number), or ISBN (International Standard Book Number)—is required to sell on Amazon. If your items are unique or you fabricate them yourself, you'll need to buy bar codes, one for each product, including variations of the same product, such as color. There are many places you can buy barcodes: three of these are speedybarcodes.com, www.barcodestalk.com, and www.gs1uk.org. You can easily find other providers and compare prices by doing a Google search.

5. If you're going to use the Fulfillment by Amazon service, you'll need to get this set up and your products shipped. If you opted for this during the registration process, you'll have received a welcome email which directs you to www.amazon.com/fba-manual. Go to this web page, scroll down, and click on the link labeled "Download the FBA Quickstart Guide." This will provide you with full instructions for printing out your product labels, preparing and labeling your shipment, and shipping your products to Amazon.

You can register for Fulfillment by Amazon at any stage by navigating to Settings > Account info at the top right of the Seller Central screen.

Setting up Fulfillment by Amazon is initially quite complex, however all the information is documented at the link above, and there is also a specific Help section for FBA (click the yellow button to the right on the referenced page), which provides a number of detailed videos.

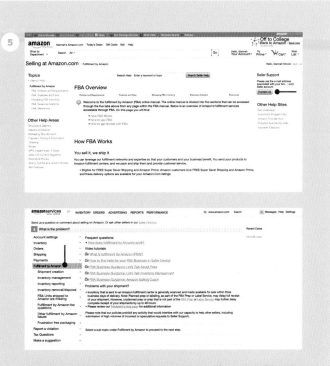

To access help videos for FBA, go to www.amazon.com/fba-manual, click on the yellow button to the right of the screen, and then on "Fulfillment by Amazon" on the left, as shown.

6. Back in your main Seller Central area (sellercentral.amazon.com), there are some settings you'll want to adjust before your storefront setup is complete. Scroll down toward the bottom of the page and click the "Account Info" link. You'll need to add your bank account information, perhaps adjust your customer service email address, provide a customer service telephone number and a returns address, and set a storefront link—this is the web address to which you direct your prospective customers, and will look like this: www.amazon.com/shops/your_chosen_name.

7. As we have emphasized, the Amazon storefront system doesn't allow for much branding of the individual sellers' storefronts, however there are various customizations you can apply to your account from within the Your Info and Policies section (down toward the bottom of the left-hand column on the Seller Central page). The system allows you to upload a logo (sized to 120 pixels wide by 30 pixels high) and you get the opportunity to provide some "about" text (as shown in the screenshot). You'll also need to add a privacy policy, and you may want to provide FAQ, custom help pages, and other information such as gift wrapping, tax policy, and shipping options.

Once you've input all your product details (and if you're using the FBA system, once your goods are shipped to Amazon's fulfillment center), you'll be in business, with millions of potential customers able to access what you're selling.

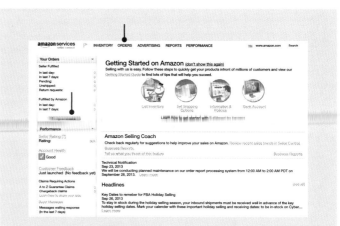

MANAGING YOUR AMAZON STOREFRONT

You can manage your orders, interact with your buyers, print your shipping labels and packing slips, update your order status and download order reports from the Orders area of Seller Central, as indicated in the screenshot above.

Getting help

It's likely you'll need guidance during the setup and the early days of running your store. Go to Seller Central (sellercentral. amazon.com) and click the "Getting Started Guide" link; this is a very helpful guide that covers what you need to know for the setup. When you need more information, you can click the help button (indicated in the screenshot) which will take you to Amazon's very thorough help documentation, the Seller Forum (sellercentral.amazon.com/forums), or to contact Amazon (sellercentral.amazon.com/gp/contact-us/contact-amazon-form.html), where you can request a telephone callback.

An eBay STOREFRONT

Like selling on Amazon, listing your products on eBay makes them available to a ready audience of millions. Why would you set up an eBay store rather than simply list your products on eBay?

There are several benefits to setting up a store:
> You'll save on listing fees.
> You're more likely to attract regular customers.
> You can refer potential customers to a single web address.
> You can customize your eBay store so that you can bring promotions to buyers' attention.
> You can create individual categories that fit the products you're selling.
> You get some great marketing tools, including an email list manager.

Sign-up requirements

You need a "Premier" or "Business" PayPal account to set up an eBay store. If you already have a Personal PayPal account, it's simple to upgrade—click "Upgrade Account" from within your PayPal admin area. You also need to get your PayPal account verified, if it isn't already. Requirements vary slightly from country to country, but verifying your account usually involves confirming a bank account. To do this, PayPal will transfer a small sum to your bank account with a series of numbers as a reference; to verify your account, you have to type in these numbers within your PayPal admin area. This can be done quickly and easily if you have internet access to your bank account.

If you want anything other than a Basic level store (150 listings a month) you can't have a seller performance from previous eBay listings that is below standard.

BEFORE YOU SET UP: BE AWARE OF SELLER LIMITATIONS

As a new seller, your account will be limited for the first 90 days; you need to build your sales and establish a good reputation for your limits to be increased. This means that it may take several months for your store to bring in a large revenue. Be aware of this when making your plans as it will prevent you growing fast if your eBay store is your only sales outlet.

OTHER PAYMENT METHODS YOU CAN USE WITH AN EBAY STORE

Skrill and ProPay are alternative payment methods you can offer to your customers from your eBay store, as well as accepting credit cards. You can't do the latter via the system, however—you need to ask your customers to contact you to complete the transaction. If it suits you, you can also offer "payment on pickup."

SETTING UP YOUR EBAY STOREFRONT

1. Go to www.ebay.com and sign in, if you're already an eBay seller, or register if you're new (the link to do this is at the very top left of your screen).

2. Go to pages.ebay.com/storefronts/start.html and look at the information about which package is right for you. Clicking the blue "Compare Packages" button will take you to a table where you can read the features of each. When you've decided which package to go for, scroll right to the bottom and click the green "Subscribe now" button.

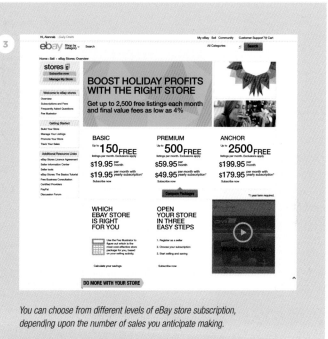

You can choose from different levels of eBay store subscription, depending upon the number of sales you anticipate making.

3. If you've just registered for a new eBay account, you'll need to confirm your contact information by phone or text, by typing the PIN number given to you into the box. You'll also need to choose the payment method with which eBay will take payment for the charges incurred by your sales, and provide them with the necessary information. When you've done this, you can go on and "Subscribe" for the store package you've decided on. You'll be giving your store a name at this stage; you can rename it any time you like, but be aware that if you rename it, the web address will also change, so think carefully and decide on a permanent name before passing on its web address to anyone, and don't change it again.

4. You've now completed the sign-up—you'll be taken to a "Congratulations" screen. Note the web address of your new store; right-click on the link, and open it in a new tab.

Your new eBay store will look rather drab, so go back to the tab in which you have the congratulations screen open and click on the blue button labeled "Start Quick Store Setup." This is a good way to get started, although you'll want to make many refinements, so scroll down to the bottom of the screen and click "Apply changes."

5. Having done this, you'll find yourself inside the Manage My Store area of My eBay (see the screenshot opposite). Here you can carry out a number of customizations:

i. From the left-hand menu, click "Display Settings" under Store Design. Here, you can change your store name, if you want to. You'll need to add a logo and change the description for your store; click the "Change" link to the right. Your description needs to include essential keywords that describe the products you sell to enable your store to be found by your prospective buyers, so think about this carefully

(see Chapter 11 for more info about the search engines).

ii. For your logo, you have the option of choosing one of eBay's pre-designed logos, but if you have your own, you'll certainly want to display it. It's important that before you do anything, you resize the image file to 310 x 90 pixels. If you don't, the image you upload will be resized to fit those dimensions and it will look either squashed or stretched. If you don't have any image-editing software

you can do this easily using Pixlr.com. Having resized the image, select the button next to "Upload a logo to eBay," and use the "Browse" and "Upload" buttons to upload your resized logo to your store. You have the option not to have a logo, but if you want to make your store look attractive, it makes sense to show a logo and choose a template (the next step) that allows you to do this (not all of them do). When you're done, click the "Save

Subscribe to eBay Store: Congratulations

You're now subscribed to the Basic Store and Selling Manager

You'll receive an email confirmation shortly. Your current active listings will appear in your new eBay store.
Your eBay store URL is: http://stores.ebay.com/alannahmoore
Your monthly subscription begins today

Quick Store Setup
Take a few minutes to use Quick Store Setup to customize your Store and create a unique shopping experience for your buyers

Start Quick Store Setup

Selling Manager
Selling Manager is a web-based sales management tool to help you manage your sales more efficiently. Please note that we are copying your eBay listings into your new tool, and they may take a few hours to appear.

Quick Store Setup
With Sales Report Plus, you can start tracking your sales activity today. Your first report will be available at the end of the first week of the following month
To view your latest report go to the "My Account" in My eBay, then select "Sales Reports". If we show that you haven't viewed your reports within 6 days, we'll assume you're not interested and discontinue the sales reports for you. You can resubscribe to Sales Reports, but you won't be able to access previous sales reports.

Settings" button at the bottom.

iii. Now, you'll want to change the "theme" (template) of your site, unless you're happy with the classic blue theme. In the Theme and Display section underneath the Basic Setting section, click "Change to another theme," select the theme you want, and click "Save Settings." You can then customize it further by changing the colors and fonts

by clicking "Edit current theme." You can change further elements of the layout in the lower part of the Theme and Display area. For example, reorganizing the content that appears in the navigation area and choosing how your products will be displayed, but this you'll find easier when you have some content on the site, such as items for sale, extra pages, categories, etc.

TIP

Customizing your header area
Your header area is a great place to feature bestselling items or links to other pages of your store. Click the "Change" button next to "Store header display" (under Theme and Display in Display Settings); click the radio button next to "Yes, include additional information in the header," and click the link labeled "Stores HTML Builder." The wizard that opens allows you to create text links or more advanced boxes that display images and text.

MANAGING YOUR EBAY STORE

There are multiple tools provided by eBay to help you manage your eBay business. If you go to My eBay you will be taken to your Selling Manager screen where you can see your listings, orders, and other information all in one place (you can also access this area from inside your Store Manager).

From here, you can download sales history reports from the File Management Center (in the left-hand navigation), print invoices and shipping labels, and if you plan to sell a large number of items from your store, sign up for Turbo Lister, which allows you to upload product information to your store in bulk.

From your Store Manager page you can sign up for traffic reports with a system called Omniture, which also allows you to see which keywords your buyers have found you with, and sign up to access detailed sales reports (subscribe to both these facilities from the bottom of the Store Manager home page).

The Selling Manager will be the center of your store management once your store is up and running.

Promoting your eBay store

You can access all kinds of marketing tools from within your Store Manager, such as promotional flyers to print out, cross-promotion tools, "Top Picks" selections, setting up an RSS feed, creating a listing frame, and the inclusion of "similar items" on customer emails and product pages. A great feature offered by an eBay store is a built-in mailing list system, allowing you to contact your email list subscribers with images of your latest products, items on sale, and so on. This is a highly effective way of staying in touch with your prospective customers and one that eBay makes very easy for you to implement. Additionally, inside the Promote Your Store area of the eBay Stores Overview (see the link in the "Getting help" box) you can generate blog widgets and download templates for business cards, letterheads, and more.

With an eBay storefront you are provided with a multitude of marketing tools, including an email mailing list system.

Getting help

There's a lot of support available to help you set up and run your eBay store. The eBay Stores Overview section is full of useful advice (pages. ebay.com/storefronts/start.html), as is the Seller Information Center (pages.ebay.com/sellerinformation/index.html). Also see the eBay University Learning Center (pages.ebay.com/education/index.html), and the Customer Support pages (ocsnext.ebay.com/ocs/home), from where you can access a customer service support telephone number and passcode.

7

In focus: webstores

A WEBSTORE IS TRULY YOUR OWN ONLINE SPACE. YOU CAN PRESENT YOUR ONLINE BUSINESS AS YOU WANT TO, YET THE BEHIND-THE-SCENES STRUCTURE IS ALREADY IN PLACE.

A *Wix* WEBSTORE

Wix is a wonderful solution, ideal for small-scale entrepreneurs. The ready-made designs are great, the interface is very easy to work with, and it's cheap. It won't be your webstore of choice if you're planning to grow your business in a big way, since the system lacks some of the more sophisticated features, such as sales reports. But for many, you won't need to look any further, and you can be up and running with a stunning-looking webstore both quickly and easily.

Wix offers a wide variety of styles so there's something for everyone. The templates are really easy to edit, as well.
Top: The Art Seller, Wooden Toys; middle: The Paperie, The Scarf Shop; bottom: Beauty Care, Jewelry Shop.

SETTING UP YOUR WIX WEBSTORE

1. Click "Templates" on Wix's home page at www.wix.com. Choose the template you want to use from the Online Shop category (clicking on "View" brings up a demo of each). You can play around with the different templates by clicking "Edit" and signing up for an account; you don't have to commit to anything at this stage. This is great because you're able to see what changes you can make to a template before you decide on it—but beware: when you do choose a template, you won't be able to change it, so make sure you've chosen well.

2. When you've chosen your template, if you haven't already clicked the "Edit" button in order to fiddle around with the site, do so now, and from the top navigation, click "Upgrade."

TIP

A unique design
If you want to create something unique, you can choose from a selection of blank layout templates and create the design yourself from scratch.

3. Name your site and save it. You need to do this, even if you haven't done anything yet, in order to upgrade. (It's not worth spending a lot of time thinking about the name you give your site as you'll be adding your own domain, so you won't be using the web address given to you by Wix.)

4. Upgrade to either the monthly or yearly e-commerce package.

5. Depending on your choice of monthly or yearly payment, your domain name may or may not be included in the price. If you've chosen to pay monthly, the final "Congratulations" screen will offer you the possibility of purchasing your domain at this point—type the domain name you want into the box and click "Search" (as shown).

6. If you've chosen to pay for the year, the price of your domain will be subtracted from your payment. To claim your free domain go to My Account and click "Domains" from the Manage Premium menu. (You can do this at any stage, but your right to claim a free domain will only last for a year.)

You must save your site before upgrade ✕

🖫 It's time to save your work and name your site

Cookery site | **Save Now**

http://alannahmoore.wix.com/cookery-site

- You can change your site name later or Connect your own personal domain i.e. (www.mydomain.com)

- Don't worry, your site is still private and will only be shown to the world when you publish it.

Not now thank you, continue editing

English ▾ | Hello m67598 log-out

Manage Premium
Packages | Domains | Mail Boxes | Vouchers

CONNECT YOUR OWN DOMAIN NOW

Enter the Domain Name you'd like for your site:

[_____] .com ▾ | **Search**
.co.uk
.com
.org
1-Year FREE domain .net
+ more gifts included with .biz
Combo/Unlimited/eCommerce Yearly Package Upgrade .info

Gift me >

WiX Templates Explore Features My Account Premium Support 🌐 English ▾

My Account | alannahsite

Manage My Site - alannahsite
Manage Premium: Packages | Domains | Mail Boxes | vouchers | Billing & Payment | Settings

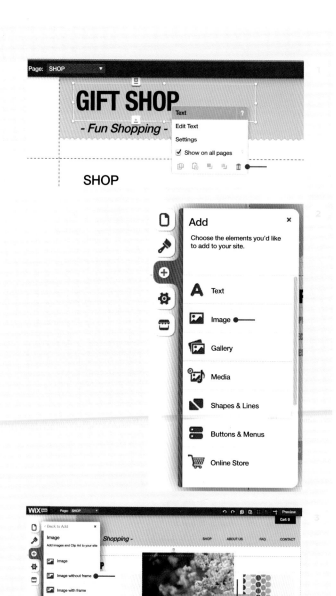

How to add your logo

One of the first things you'll probably want to do is add your own logo to replace the heading supplied with your template. Using this template as an example, here's how to do it.

1. First you need to delete the words "Gift Shop" (or whatever words you have at the top of your template), so click on the text and then the dustbin in the box of options that comes up (as shown).

2. Next, click on the "+" button on the left, and click "Image," then "Image without Frame."

3. An image will appear on your page, so click on it, and select "Change Image" from the small window that pops up.

4. Now click the orange "Upload Images" button in the large window that appears (as shown). Navigate to the image on your computer and select it. Back in the uploading window, click on your image when it has uploaded, and then click the blue "Change Image" button at the bottom right of the window. Note that you will need to use a version of your logo with a transparent background, unless its background matches exactly with the background color of

the area of your site in which you want it to appear. You may also need to resize it for your site—it's easy to do this if necessary using Pixlr.com (see page 42).

5. You now have your logo on the site but it will be the wrong size on the page—you want it to be exactly the same size as the image file you uploaded so that it does not appear distorted. Double-click on the logo as it is on the page, and the large window opens again. Mouse over the magnifying glass at the bottom left of the logo image and you can see the size of the image file—here it's 333 x 37 pixels. Click the "x" at the top right of the window to close it.

6. Now click once on the oversized logo and choose "Settings" from the small window that appears. Add the correct pixel sizes in the boxes in the Image Settings pane (as shown), hit "Enter," and the logo will resize.

7. Once your logo is resized, just move it to the right place. Note that it's a good idea to keep a descriptive subheading written in text beneath your logo, because the search engines will be able to read it.

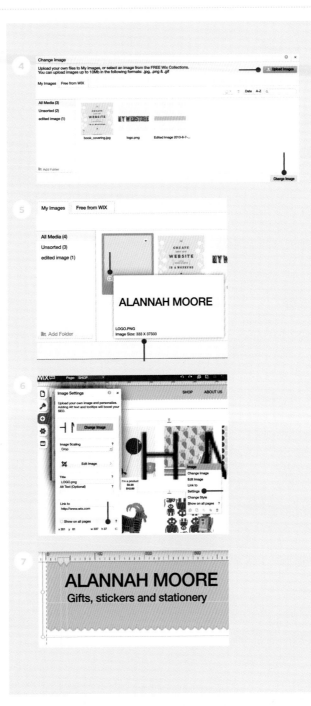

ADDING YOUR PRODUCTS AND MANAGING YOUR ORDERS

Just like the rest of the interface, the online shop is very easy to work with.

To add the store to your site, you need to add a product gallery from the Online Store section of the "+" menu, from which your customers can choose the items they want to purchase. In order to allow them to make their purchases, you need to create a page for the Shopping Cart, also in the Online Store section. If you've chosen an e-commerce template, your site will already be set up with these, together with a "View Cart" button, which shows the number of items in the cart and allows customers to click on it to access the Shopping Cart page, from where they check out. "Add to Cart" buttons are optional as your products will already be listed in the product gallery, but you can add these in other places. For example, if you are profiling a product on a page elsewhere on the site, it makes sense to add an "Add to Cart" button at the bottom of the description.

Note that the product gallery and the product pages can be styled in different ways—bigger images, different layouts, frames around the images, and many other customizations. Click on the product gallery to access these styling options.

You can access your Store Manager in several ways. From within the page editing area, by clicking "Online Store" from the "+" in the left-hand menu of the editing screen, then "Product Gallery." You'll be provided with a "Go to Manage Store" link (or you can click on the product gallery on the page itself and then "Manage Store"). Or, from your Site Manager page, by clicking "Online Store" from the left-hand menu (you'll have to scroll down the page a little to see it).

Getting help with Wix

Wix has a very clear and informative Learning Center, complete with videos. Click Support at the top right of the main part of the site. There's also a support forum. Clicking the small "Contact Us" link in the footer of each page in the main part of the site will bring you to a page with a toll-free U.S. number and an international number for telephone support.

WIXSTORE Manage Your Online Store

Orders | **My Products** | **Payment & Currency** | **Coupons** | **Shipping** | **Tax**

Collections ?

Add and manage the collections your products will be displayed in.

All Products (23)

Wallpapers (9)

Stickers (7)

Cardboards (7)

Shop (23)

+ Add Collection

Important

These items may require further attention

Out of Stock (1)

Offline (1)

Uncategorized (0)

Get a FREE Facebook Store

All Products (23)

Manage products in your store from here. Click on a product to edit it. Navigate between collections using the links on the left.
It's easy to reorder products within a collection by dragging them.

Search

+ Add Product

	I'm a product	45	45	$ 9.99	>
	I'm a product	70	70	$ 9.99	>
	I'm a product	0	0	$ 9.99	>
	I'm a product	10	10	$ 9.99	>
	I'm a product	5	5	$ 9.99	>
	I'm a product	5	5	$ 9.99	>

Back to the Editor

The Store Manager works like this.

1. All your products are listed here. To edit one, click on it. Products can be reordered simply by dragging them.

2. Add a new product by clicking this button.

3. Duplicating a product, then editing it, is an easy way to create similar product listings.

4. Products need to belong to collections. Product galleries on the site display one collection at a time. Products can belong to more than one collection. To add a new collection, click the "Add Collection" button.

5. You can keep track of your orders here.

6. Set your currency (just one per site) and your payment details here. At present, PayPal, Authorize.net, Skrill, WebMoney, and PagSeguro are supported. You also choose your weight unit here, either in pounds or kilos, for shipping purposes.

7. Here is where you create product coupons to give your customers special discounts.

8. Set your shipping rules here: where are you going to ship to, are you going to calculate shipping by weight or price,

and are you going to set a handling fee?

9. Set your tax rules here: is tax included in your pricing, for which countries is it applicable, and what percentage is it?

10. This area brings products to your attention that may be out of stock, not visible on the site, or not classed into any collection.

11. This link allows you to sign up to display your online store on Facebook, complete with purchase buttons.

The Product Details interface works like this. (It is accessed by clicking on a product within the Store Manager.)

1. Product title and the price at which it will be sold.

2. Choose the collection(s) to which the product will be added.

3. You can add multiple photos and videos for each product.

4. The "Overview" information appears at the top of the product page, the "Detail" information will appear at the bottom.

5. You can optionally add text that will appear on a strip of color on the product image in the product gallery.

6. If you want a crossed-out price to appear next to the current price, type it here. If you put "0," nothing will show up.

7. If you've set the system to calculate shipping costs by weight, you need to add the product weight in this box (this is set under the "Shipping" tab in the Store Manager).

8. Here is where you can manage options, such as size and color (two are allowed for each product), and the quantity of each product you have in stock.

9. Here is where you can temporarily remove an item from the gallery, for example, if it's out of stock.

10. Don't forget to save the product details.

A *Shopify* WEBSTORE

If you need more sophisticated features than Wix can offer you, consider Shopify. Shopify's templates are some of the most stunning around, and the easy-to-use interface makes it a breeze to set one up.

The system can also be extended with hundreds of apps to increase functionality, and you can integrate it with various dropshipping and fulfillment systems.

Shopify has the best selection of ready-made webstore templates ("themes") around, with slick designs to suit every type of site. Top: Masonry theme (Chameleon), Limitless theme (Methods); bottom: Radiance theme (Slate), Clean theme (Colour).

SETTING UP YOUR SHOPIFY WEBSTORE

1. First, sign up for a free 14-day trial at www.shopify.com. Input your store name (which can be changed later), your email address, desired password, and click "Create your store now." You'll need to wait while your new store is created, then click "Take me to my store."

2. Supply your address as requested, click the "I'm done" button, and proceed to your Dashboard. You'll see three steps listed on the Dashboard home screen that you need to follow for your site to be functional. If you want to see what your store looks like, click on the green button labeled "View your store" at the top of the screen, which will open in a new tab. This way you can work in the admin area and check your changes on the site in a separate tab (refreshing your browser each time you make a change). As you scroll down the site, you'll see customization suggestions appearing in yellow boxes as you mouse over the different areas—don't follow these. It's easier to follow the three-step setup from the admin area, plus you'll probably want to change the theme (template), in any case.

3. The first thing to do is customize your theme. You may want to change the theme—this you can do straight away by clicking the "Visit the Theme Store" link. Alternatively, you may want to play around a little with the default theme first, in order to familiarize yourself with the way Shopify works.

To customize the default theme click on "Edit theme." From within this area, you can make a huge number of customizations. Not only can you change colors, fonts, and background, and upload a logo, you can add a slideshow, and choose what content appears where on your home page. Here, you also configure your mailing list settings and decide which social media buttons you want on your product pages. (You will need to scroll right down the page and open each menu item.)

You'll see that you can also make some choices relating to the display of your products, but this won't really make sense until you've added some in the next step, so you'll want to come back here when you've done that. (To come back here, click "Themes" from the left-hand navigation and then "Theme Settings"—don't click on "Template Editor," as this is where you or a developer, would make changes to the code.)

When you've made these customizations, saved them, and checked how they look on your live site, return to your Dashboard by clicking the "Dashboard" link on the left-hand navigation.

If you want to change themes at any later stage, click "Themes" from the left-hand navigation and then "Visit the Theme Store" from the top right corner of the screen.

4. Back at the Dashboard, which now tells you you've customized your store, scroll down the page to the second step and click "Add Products." Now, click the green "Add a product" button, as directed. Add your product information and images, grouping them into collections as you wish. (You can create new collections in the Collections area—click "Collections" in the left-hand navigation.)

If you have your product details ready, a fast way of uploading them is via a spreadsheet. Click "Products" from the left-hand navigation and then the "Import Products" button at the top right of the screen. Download the sample spreadsheet, input your own product information, and upload the completed spreadsheet to your store.

Note that you will need to choose which products you want to appear on the home page, and add them to the "Frontpage" collection.

When you've added as many products as you want to at this stage, click "Dashboard."

Working with images

You can add images to your site either by uploading them from your computer or directly from the web. To get an image from the web, navigate to the image in question, right-click on the image and choose "View image" or "Open image in new tab." Then copy the web address of the image, and paste it into the window in Shopify that appears when you click on "add images from the web" (the upper arrow in the screenshot). The image now resides on your own webstore system.

Shopify also has a useful built-in image editing feature (as shown) that allows you to resize, rotate, crop, add text, alter colors, etc. To access it, click on the small pencil (the lower arrow in the screenshot). Clicking on the "alt" label allows you to add keywords that will be visible to a viewer who can't access images on their computer; this is very rare these days, but this information has value for the search engines, so do take the trouble to type a keyword in here. Images can be reordered by dragging them, and deleted by clicking the trash icon.

5. The third step in the quick setup is to configure your domain name. If you are ready to do this, click the "Add a domain" button (you'll have to scroll down the page to see it). Click the "Buy domain" button at the top right of the screen to register a new domain name via Shopify, or if you already have a domain name that you want to point to your Shopify store, click the "Add existing domain" button. Type in your domain name, click "Add domain," then "Go to instructions," and follow the instructions Shopify gives you to point your domain to your store for your particular domain registrar. It can take up to 24 hours for the change to take effect, but during this time, you can continue to work on your store.

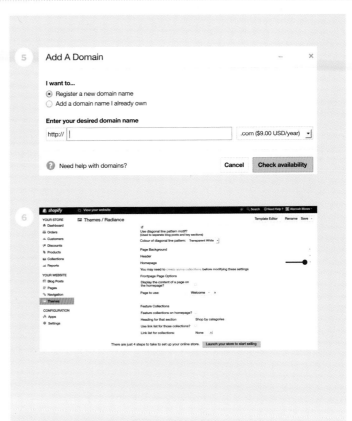

6. You're through with the three-step quick setup, but there are other settings that need to be configured. You'll need to set up your tax and shipping rates—these you access via the "Settings" link at the bottom of the left-hand navigation. (If you need to consult the Help area, click "Need help?" from the top right of your screen, then "Shopify Help Center.")

Note that if you are going to use a dropshipping or order fulfillment service, such as Fulfillment by Amazon, you can configure your dropshipping or fulfillment settings from within the Shipping area. You may also want to change the currency or the unit system, which can be done within Settings > General.

7. Now you need to set up your payment system(s). This is done under Settings > Checkout. The options you have available to you vary depending on where you are based. North American users have the option of using Shopify Payments to collect credit and debit card payments. You can activate any of the other payment gateways available in your country by using the "Choose a Credit Card Gateway" drop-down menu. As discussed previously, you may choose to launch your store using PayPal only and sign up for an alternative payment system later.

PayPal Express checkout is a default payment system with Shopify. As soon as you receive your first order, PayPal will send you an email instructing you how to complete your PayPal Express setup. If you want to use a different type of PayPal payment system, just deactivate the PayPal Express Checkout setting. Click Edit > Deactivate (it can be reactivated later, if you want) and choose the PayPal system you want to use from the "Select a Payment Method" drop-down. Complete the setup by following the instructions in the pane that opens up

and completing the fields as required. In addition, you can choose Cash on Delivery, Money Order, or Bank Deposit from the "Custom Payment Method" drop-down.

SSL AND SHOPIFY
There is no need to purchase a separate SSL (secure sockets layer, see page 33) as you'll be using the Shopify checkout, which is protected by its own SSL. It may add extra customer reassurance to see that an entire site is protected by https://, however adding a custom SSL is not an option with Shopify at present.

8. When you've configured your means of collecting payment from your webstore, scroll further down the page. Under the "Customer accounts" heading, choose whether you wish customers to sign up for an account with you. The next section, "Order Processing" allows you to make some choices about how checkout and payment processing occurs. You may need to consult the "Help" section here as some of the options are a little complicated—click the "Learn about order processing" link to the left.

9. Finally in this area, you will need to configure the text for your Refund, Privacy, and Terms of Service statements. Clicking the "Generate…" buttons to the left populates the fields with standard text that you may find useful as a basis from which to create your own. When you've done this, click the "Save Changes" button at the bottom.

10. You are through with the basic setup walkthough, but there is other customization to be done before your site goes live:

> **adding pages to the site**
> **attaching these pages to a menu for the site**
> **adding "link lists" to your site (These are mini-menus. You can also create drop-down menus this way. Create a link list with the same name and "handle" as the main menu item you want it to appear under, and it will appear as a drop-down menu beneath it.)**
> **adding blog posts to the site**
> **editing the emails customers will receive when they make a purchase, if wanted (Settings > Notifications)**
> **setting up discount codes (Discounts area in the admin menu)**

Congratulations! Your webstore is now live. Enjoy using Shopify!

Extras to add to your Shopify store

You can add to the functionality of your Shopify store by installing different apps, some of which are free, others paid for on a monthly basis. Access the App Store, where you can browse the list of available apps, by clicking on Apps > Visit the App Store. Some of the most popular are:

Chimpified—integrate your MailChimp email list manager with Shopify (free)

Product Upsell—suggest tempting last-minute offers to your customers (premium)

Yotpo Social Reviews—generate reviews you can share on social media (free)

ShopPad—make your store even more beautiful and accessible on a tablet by generating a flippable catalog (free)

Product Discount—schedule daily deals and timed sales (premium)

Product Bundles—bundle products together and create discounts to increase your overall sales (premium)

Beetailer—integrate your store with Facebook (premium)

Abandon Aid—automatically email customers who abandon the checkout process at the last moment, reminding them to come back to the order and complete it (premium)

Email Template Creator—make your Shopify emails look great (free)

Retail Tower—list your products on shopping comparison engines (free)

Ordoro—inventory control across Shopify, eBay, and Amazon; batch and dropshipping management (premium)

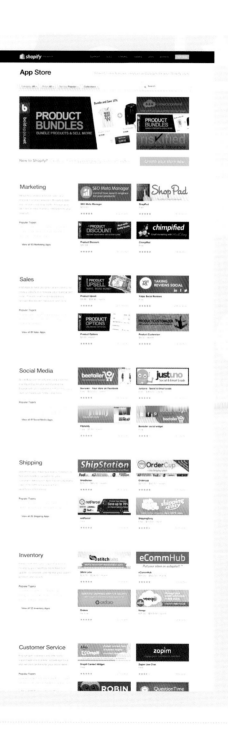

Getting help with Shopify

The support available from Shopify is excellent. Click the "Need help?" link at the top right of your admin screen. From there, you can access Live Chat, email support, or call a support number local to where you are. You can also access a knowledge base, a series of manuals including a useful "Building Your Store" manual, and a discussion forum. Clicking "Forums" from the support area takes you to a new section entitled "Ecommerce University." Within this section, you can read success stories and access a free store grader, whereby you can submit your store for analysis and receive feedback on how it can be improved. Finally, clicking "Learning" allows you to access mentor archives, an "Ecommerce 101" video series, a business plan guide, and "The Ultimate Guide to Dropshipping"—a depth of information to plumb for those getting started with their online business.

Shopify provides a great information resource for those getting started with an online business.

A *Bigcommerce* WEBSTORE

Bigcommerce is a full-featured system that offers multiple "bells and whistles" right out of the box. The designs have a different look and feel to Shopify's, so it's really a matter of listing your needs, comparing who can provide what at what cost, and then making a decision in terms of budget and appearance. Note that the templates are not customizable without going into the coding.

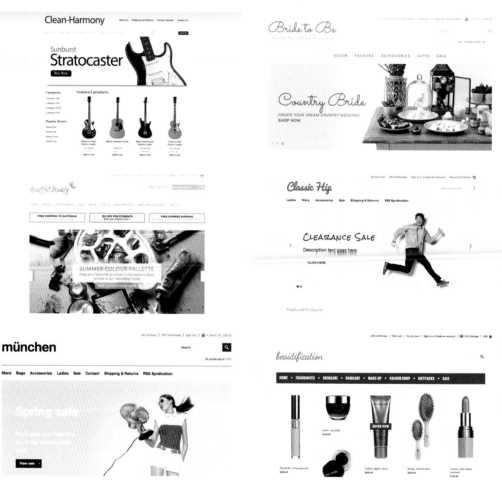

All the Bigcommerce templates available from within the interface are free. You can't make simple changes, such as to colors or fonts, without going into the coding, so choose one you are completely happy with if you don't want to have to call on a programmer. Top: Clean-Harmony, Bride to Be; middle: Health and Beauty, Classic Hip; bottom: München, Beautification.

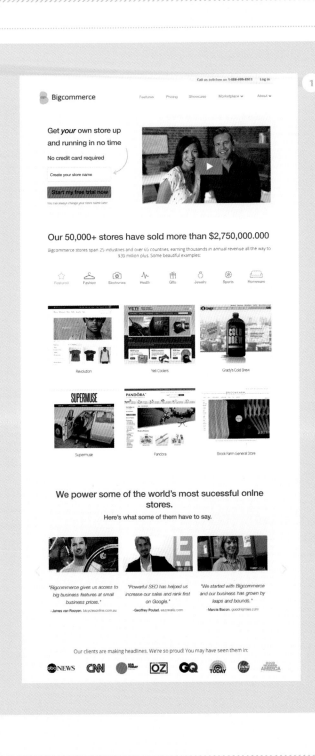

SETTING UP YOUR BIGCOMMERCE WEBSTORE

1. Type in your store name (which you can always change) and click the orange "Start my free trial now" button.

2. Type in some basic details and wait for your store to be built.

3. When you see the "Now Open" sign, you can click the button and access the admin area of your new store.

The Quick Start Wizard guides you through the setup. At any point in the setup you can return to the Wizard by clicking the tab at the top of the screen.

1. Step one of the Wizard is the basic customization of the site. Click "Change your design theme and add a logo," then the "Change your theme and logo" button. Choose your template by trying them out—very little customization is possible without going into the coding, so make sure there's a template there you're really happy with just as it is.

2. Click on the "Logo" tab and either upload your logo, or change the title of the webstore, if you need to.

3. While you're in this area, although you could always do this later, you can change your mobile settings. It's a good idea to enable your shop on tablet devices as well as on phones, and upload a smaller-sized logo to appear on the mobile version of the webstore. All Bigcommerce stores have a mobile version that is clear and easy to use, but the design is the same for all themes, meaning your branding is restricted to the logo.

The Quick Start Wizard helps you get set up quickly and easily.

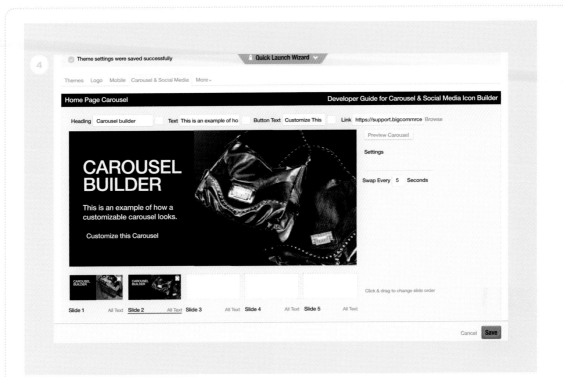

4. While you're here, customize your carousel, if your template includes one. Bigcommerce lets you add up to five slides to the home page carousel. Prepare your images in advance using Pixlr.com or any other image-editing software; they need to be sized at 980 pixels wide x 450 pixels high. (These sizes work for any of the templates that use a carousel—the system will resize them as necessary to fit the template.) Click the large rectangular area to browse for the prepared images on your computer, or simply drag them into this area. Add headings, smaller text, and button text as required; you can change the color of this text by clicking the small squares next to the fields, which brings up a color picker. You'll find it easier to come back later and add the "destination links"—these are the web pages you want the user to be directed to when they click on the images, so you'll need to have some real website content in place first. (Note that to delete a slider, click the small gray "x" top right of the thumbnail version of the image).

CHOOSING YOUR CURRENCY
Go to Setup & Tools at the top right of your screen, and click "Currency" to add currencies and choose your default. You can either manually input an exchange rate, or use the Bigcommerce Currency service—if you want to use the latter, check the radio button and a "Get Rate" button will appear. Click it and the exchange rate will appear in the box. (You can get three-letter currency codes here: www.xe.com/iso4217.php)

5. Now, scroll down a little and choose which social media buttons you want to appear on your site. You can choose between the standard icons with logos on them, and specially designed icons that go with the theme. Click "Save" when you've finished making changes to this section.

6. The "More" tab allows you to access "Design Mode," which is a way of letting you change text on the site easily, and move the content panels around.

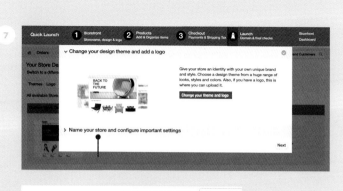

The other elements underneath the "More" tab allow you to access the content of emails that get sent out to clients, and gift certificates, as well as allowing you access to the template files so that changes can be made to your design and layout. You need to know how to code to edit these, so you probably won't be going into these files yourself, but if you ever employ a programmer to work on your site, here is where these edits can be carried out.

Changes you may want to make yourself from this section would be the header images, if your chosen template has one—you would

download it, edit it and upload the new version within the Header area—and a "favicon," which is the tiny image (16 x 16 pixels) you can see to the left of each browser page title at the top of your screen. It's worth creating one and adding it via the Favicon area, as it adds to your overall professionalism and branding.

7. Click the "Quick Launch Wizard" tab at the top of the screen and click the link that says "Name your store and configure important settings;" then the blue button that

says "Update your store settings."

This area—navigate as before, moving from tab to tab—is where you set your basic settings and make other more complex decisions about the layout and functionality of the site, as well as configuring social media and SEO (see Chapters 11 and 12). There are numerous features to be configured, each with an explanation displayed when you click on the "i" next to it. Click "Save" when you've finished. (You can return to this section by clicking "Setup & Tools" at the top right corner of your screen, then "Store settings" underneath "Customize your store.")

8. Go to the Quick Launch tab again, click "Next," and then "Add products."

The Products section is where you add your products, with their details, images, weight, and so on; configure options such as size and color; set custom fields; add SKUs (stock keeping units) and product codes; activate Google Shopping (see page 164); specify shipping costs; add keywords and descriptions for SEO; and so on. If you have a large number of products, these can be imported via a CSV file. Go to Products > Import Products from the main menu.

When you've added your products, it's easy to manage them from the View Products screen (Products > View Products). You can see stock levels, prices, and codes at a glance, select which products are displayed as "Featured," and, using the links across the top of the table, see which ones offer free shipping, which ones are out of stock, which ones are "hidden" on the site, etc. Once you've linked the system with your eBay account, you can even list the products on eBay from this screen.

9. When you've finished adding products for now, go to the Quick Launch tab and click the "Next" button. Click "Accept online payments" and then "Setup payment methods." Once you've chosen your payment systems, you'll see them appear as tabs. Click on the tabs and configure each one individually. When you've finished, click "Save."

Note that the recommended PayPal system for use with Bigcommerce is PayPal Express Checkout. You can also use PayPal Website Payments (Standard) by selecting it from the "More payment methods" box— you'll need to do this if for the time being PayPal is your only means of accepting payment.

10. Go back to the Quick Launch tab and configure your shipping and tax settings— if you need help, see the box below.

11. Click on the Quick Launch tab one more time and click "Next"—you've now finished the basic setup. You can click the orange button and launch your store. If you've successfully completed all the steps, your store is now open and you'll see a large "Open" sign appear.

Of course, there is more customization that you'll want to do. For example, you'll want to add some more pages to your site.

Getting help with shipping and tax settings
There are articles to help with both these in the Bigcommerce knowledge base. Click "Help" at the top right of your admin screen, then "Getting Started" underneath "Browse by Category;" you'll see articles here labeled "How do I set up shipping zones and methods?" and "How do I set up my tax settings?"

Adding pages to your site

You'll certainly want to add pages to your site: Terms & Conditions, FAQ, About Us, etc. Here's how to do it.

1. Go to Web Content > Create a Web Page.

2. Click the radio button next to "This Page Will Contain content created using the WYSIWYG editor below."

3. Type your page title in the field labeled "Page Name;" no need to write anything in the "Page URL" field as this will be filled in automatically. Type whatever content you like into the "Page Content" field. You can also add images or videos by using the buttons indicated in the screenshot.

   Supposing you wanted to write a different, perhaps more succinct version for people browsing your website on a smartphone or tablet; you'd check the checkbox next to "Mobile Version" and fill in your alternative text in the new field that appears. Of course, you can switch the mobile version on or off, as we saw during the setup— you can go back to that area by clicking "Design" at the top right of your screen.

TIP

Connecting a blog to your Bigcommerce store

As mentioned, there's no integral blog with Bigcommerce, but you can connect an external blog (e.g. on WordPress.com or Blogger) to the menu so your visitors can access it directly. Go to Web Content > Create a Web Page and select "Link to another website or document." Type the link title as you'd like it to appear in the menu (e.g."Blog"), paste in the web address of your blog, and click "Save & Exit." Alternatively, you can map your blog to a subdomain of your store domain. It will look something like blog.yourdomain. com. For instructions on how to do this, go to the knowledge base and search "subdomain blog," and you'll find links to articles explaining how to do this with both WordPress and Blogger.

Getting help with Bigcommerce

To access the support area, click "Help" at the top right of the admin screen. From this area you can access Live Chat, phone for support, or send a support ticket. There is also a knowledge base, a forum, and a series of videos; in addition, Bigcommerce runs "webinars" you can sign up for if you have questions you want to ask, or watch pre-recorded webinars on topics such as content marketing, website conversion, and Search Engine Optimization.

E-commerce webinars from Bigcommerce are a fount of information on online business in general, as well as on the system itself.

DOMAINS AND SSL

When you're ready to add your own domain to your webstore, you can either purchase one through Bigcommerce, or you can link up a domain you've already registered with a different registrar. Go to Setup & Tools from the top right of your admin area, and click either "Buy a new domain name" or "Use an existing domain name." Follow the instructions. If you have a domain registered elsewhere, you will need to log in and change the nameservers to "ns1.bigcommerce.com" and "ns2.bigcommerce.com." (If you need help with this, go to the support area and search "nameservers" for more specific instructions.)

You do not need to purchase an SSL to start selling on Bigcommerce, as your checkout will be protected by a shared SSL. If you want to purchase a custom SSL, or use one you already have, you have that option. Go to "Setup & Tools" and click on "SSL certificate."

A *Volusion* WEBSTORE

Volusion is an extremely full-featured, professional online store system that offers pretty much all the functionality you could ever imagine needing for your webstore.

Two factors set it apart from the other systems we look at in this book. Firstly, it isn't designed to be particularly intuitive to work with; you'll find you do have to edit some code through the admin interface in order to customize it with your own content. It is certainly possible for someone to set it up without knowing how to code, however, otherwise we wouldn't be including it in this book. This is thanks to Volusion's documentation which is very thorough, complete with videos and useful "help" links from each page. If you sign up for the free trial, which allows you to access all the features of the highest level package (except the Customer Relationship Management center), you will be able to see whether this is a system that you want to work with. Also note that the templates come with enough ready-made content that you can simply adjust, rather than build your pages entirely from scratch.

Secondly, while you should be able to get your webstore in place over the course of a weekend, you won't actually be able to go live with it so soon. This is because in order to take transactions from your site, you need to purchase an SSL (see page 33), which Volusion will install for you. This is a process that can take 7–10 days, so if you need to be able to take payment sooner than this time, Volusion won't be the system for you.

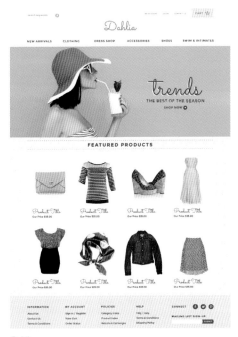

Dahlia

Collection

Chapter

Sideburns

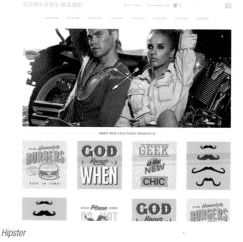

Hipster

Hardy

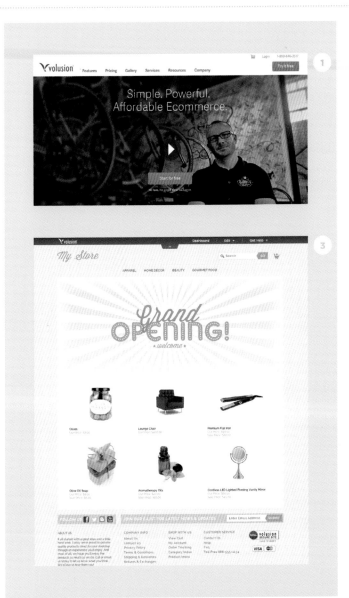

SETTING UP YOUR VOLUSION WEBSTORE

1. Go to www.volusion.com and click the "Try it Free" button at the top right.

2. Fill in your information and click "Start my Trial."

3. Wait a little while your trial site is built. When it's finished, you'll find yourself at an attractive-looking storefront, which uses one of Volusion's basic templates. Note that the store is already set up with dummy information and products.

   The Quick Start tab at the bottom allows you to switch to other free templates, add your logo, and add some products quickly and easily, which gives you a good idea of how it is going to look. If you want to purchase a premium template, click the link to the Template Gallery that you'll see when looking though the free templates inside the Quick Start tab (or select the "Website Design" menu item underneath "Edit" in the top navigation) and add your premium template to your site.

WHEN CHOOSING A TEMPLATE...

Be aware that these templates are not designed to be customizable from the admin area. As with Bigcommerce, to make "simple" changes, such as to fonts or colors, you'll either have to go into the code of the template, or get someone else to.

Changing elements on the site, changing text on pages, and adding pages

Volusion has an "on-page editing" feature which makes editing content that already exists relatively easy. Click "Edit" from the top navigation and check "Enable on-page editing." You'll now find that when you mouse over the different elements of the site, a blue box and an "Edit" button appear, as you can see in the screenshot below.

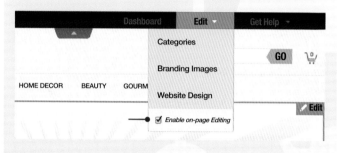

Despite it being easy to access the changeable elements, it isn't always that obvious how to proceed from clicking the "Edit" button. We'll run through some of the elements you'll certainly want to change and see exactly how it can be done. (These kinds of customizations are likely to be similar, regardless of which template you choose for your store.)

First off, let's change the image on the front page.

1. First, you need to resize the image you want to put on the home page, outside the system. If you upload a picture with different dimensions, it won't fit into the layout. You can use any image editing software to do this, or Pixlr.com. The easiest way to see the size of the existing image is to open it in a new browser window—in Firefox, for example, you can see the dimensions of the image written at the top of the screen, as shown.

2. With on-page editing enabled, click on the "Edit" button at the top right of the image on the home page.

3. In the window that pops up, click "Easy Editor."

4. In the editing window, click first on the image, and then on the small graphic showing a picture towards the top of the window (as indicated).

5. In the next small window, click on the button to the right of the field labeled "Source."

6. Click on "Choose File," navigate to the image you want to upload, select it, and click "upload."

7. Allow it to upload and then click "ok."

8. Now click "ok" in the window beneath.

9. Click "Copy HTML to parent window."

10. Finally, click "Apply," then "OK."

11. Allow the browser window to refresh, and you will see your new image on your home page.

Now let's see how you can change the text at the bottom of the pages. Even if you want to keep the links to most of the pages which have been created for you, you'll certainly want to add your own "About Us" text and change the customer support number.

1. Click the "Edit" button that appears at the top right of the "About Us" text when you mouse over it.

2. Now, edit the text in the box that comes up. Here, you can see HTML code, but you don't have to touch it. As a simple rule, don't ever touch anything in these editing boxes that's in purple, and be extremely careful when you have to change something that's in red. You'll usually be making changes to code that's written in black, as it's the black part that shows up as text on the page. So, in this instance, remove the black text that's indicated, and type in something of your own. When you're done, click "Apply." Allow the page to refresh, and you'll see your own text appearing on your home page.

(2) **Edit Region – Footer Text**

```
1
2        <span class="title">About Us</span>
3        <p>It all started with a great idea and a little hard work.
4
```

Cancel   **Apply**

(4) **Edit Region – Link Column 3**

```
1
2        <li class="title">Customer Service </li>
3        <li><a href="mailto:Config_EmailAddress_From?subject=Contact Us" title="Cc
4        <li><a href="Config_FullStoreURLhelp.asp" title="Site Help">Help</a></li>
5        <li><a href="Config_FullStoreURLhelp.asp" title="Site FAQ">Faq</a></li>
6        <li> Toll Free 888-555-1234 </li>
7
```

Cancel   **Apply**

3. Now, you'll want to change the customer support number. Click on the "Edit" button that appears when you mouse over that area.

4. Just as before, alter the black text as necessary. (Don't be alarmed that you can see more code in this window than you did for the last change we made—you're only going to change what's written in black.) Click "Apply" as before, and allow the page to refresh before checking the change you've made.

To edit a page that's already been created for you, for example the "Terms & Conditions:"

1. Navigate to that page on the site and with on-page editing active, click the "Edit" button at the top right.

2. A window will open, as before, but when you're editing an entire page rather than just a small element, you'll have the option of accessing an HTML editor to make the formatting easier. So, click the button that says "Easy Editor," as shown in the screenshot.

3. Now, edit the text as you need to within the HTML editor, using the two rows of buttons to help you with the formatting, and when you're done, click the "Copy HTML to parent window" button.

Article Editor

are free of viruses or other harmful components. $(Comany Name legal) does not make any warrantees or representations regarding the use of the materials in this site in terms of their correctness, accuracy, adequacy, usefulness, timeliness, reliability or otherwise. Some stats do not permit limittins or exclusions on warranties, so the above limitations may not apply to you.

<strong> Limitation of Liability </strong>
-$(CompanyNameLegal) shall not be liable for any special or consequential damages that result from the use of, or the inability to use, the materials on this site ir the performance of the products, even if $(Company Name Legal) has been advised of the possibility of such damages. Applicable law may not allow the limitation of exclusion of liability or incidental or consequential damages, so the above limitation or exclusion may not apply to you

 ≤strong> Typographical Errors</strong>
-In the event that a $(Company Name Legal) product is mistakenly listed at an incorrect price, $(Company Name Legal) reserves the right to refuse or cancel any orders placed for product listed at the incorrect price. $(Company Name Legal) reserves the right to refuse or cancel any such orders whether or not the order has been confirmed and your credit card charged. If your credit card has already been charged for the purchase your order is cancelled, $(Company Name Legal) shall issue a credit to your credit card account in the amount of the incorrect price

<strong> Term: Termination</strong>
 These terms and conditions are applicable to you upon your accessing the site and/or completing the registration or shopping process. These terms and conditions, or any part of them, may be terminated by $(Company Name Legal) without notice at any time for any reason. The provisions relating to Copyrights, Trademark, Disclaimed, Limitation of Liability, Indemnification and Miscellaneous...

Easy Editor

See all text in "Articles"
Edit article details

Cancel **Apply**

PLEASE READ THE FOLLOWING TERMS AND CONDITIONS OF USE CAREFULLY BEFORE USING THIS WEBSITE. All users of this site agree that access to and use of this site are subject to the following terms and conditions and other applicable law. If you do not agree to these terms and conditions, please do not use this site.

Copyright

The entire content included in this site, including but not limited to text, graphics or code is copyrighted as a collective work under the United States and other copyright laws and is the property of $(Company Name Legal). The collective work includes works that are licensed to $(Company Name Legal). Copyright 2003, $(Company Name Legal) and ALL RIGHTS RESERVED. Permission is granted to electronically copy and rpint hard copy portions of this site for the sole purpose of placing an order wi th $(Company Name Legal) or purchasing $(Company Name Legal) products. You may display and, subject to any expressly stated restrictions or limitations relating to specific material, download or print portions of the material from the different areas of the site solely for your own non-commercial use, or to place an order with $(Company Name Legal) or to purchase $(Company Name Legal) products. Any other use,

Copy HTML to parent window
(NOTE: To save you must click save changes on the main parent window afterwards)

4. Click "Apply," then "OK." This editing window only allows you to change the body text of the page. If you need to change the title, click "Edit article details" seen toward the bottom right of the screenshot. Edit the title and "caption" (subtitle) from there, clicking the orange "Save" button when you're finished. Having done this, don't forget to return to the storefront editor and save your changes to the body text.

To create an entirely new page, the process is a little more complex as you'll have to create the page from scratch.

1. Go to Dashboard > Design > Site Content.

2. Click the "View List" button toward the top right of your screen (you may need to scroll right to see it), and from the next screen, click the "Add" button.

3. Complete the "Article Title" and (optionally) the "Article Caption" (subtitle) fields. Next to the large "Article Body" area, click the "HTML Editor" link, add your text, images, etc., formatting it as you require using the row of buttons. Click the "Copy HTML to parent window" to insert this content into the main page.

4. Select "Other Articles" from the "Category ID" drop-down.

5. Click the orange "Save" button at the bottom of the page.

6. Scroll back to the top and click the "View Live Article Page" link; you'll now see the page as it appears on your site. In order for your site visitors to access it, you'll need to add a link to it. In order to do this, copy the last

part of the web address of the page—it will be something like "Articles.asp?ID=251" (as shown in the screenshot). Paste it into a text file to keep it safe for a moment.

7. Now go to the storefront and navigate to the group of links you want to add the link to the new page to. Here, I'm adding it to the group of links underneath the heading "Company Info," and I'm going to add it to the bottom of the list. Click the "Edit" button so that the window with the code appears.

8. Carefully copy the entire last line of the code (line 10) and paste it in, so that you have two identical lines of code, as shown.

9. Very carefully edit the new line you have added, line 11, as follows: Replace **Config_ FullStoreURLreturns.asp** with the part of the URL you saved in the text file earlier. Replace **Returns and Exchanges** with the title of the new page, and finally, replace **Returns & Exchanges** again with the title of the new page.

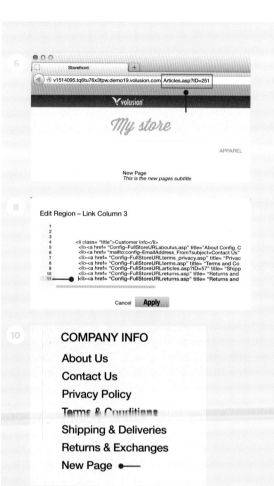

Your line of code will now look something like: **<li><a href="Articles. asp?ID=251" title="New Page">New Page</a></li>**

10. Click the green "Apply" button; you will now see the link to the new page added to the list of links.

Adding your products and setting up the store

Clicking Dashboard > Inventory > Products will take you to the Products area, where you can see the sample products Volusion has put in for you. Clicking "Enable Quick Edit" from the Settings drop-down (as shown) will enable you to edit items from a split screen interface (also shown), without having to open a separate window for each product you want to edit. If you can't see anything to edit once you enable Quick Edit, drag the dark blue bar down with your mouse and click on the product you want to edit.

From within the Products area, you can add product details, price, weight, inventory details, shipping details, multiple images and videos, and unlimited options such as size, color, etc., as well as keywords, meta tags, and descriptions for the search engines.

TIP

Deleting sample products

To add your own products, you'll need to delete the products Volusion has put in for you. You can do this by doing a "bulk" delete; click the checkbox next to "Delete" at the top of the table, and then click the orange "Save" button. However, since the system is complex, it may be helpful to keep some of these items to look at how they are set up. To do this, use the "Hidden" feature—click on "Edit" under "Hidden" to enable it, then select the items you want to hide and click "Save."

Your company details, shipping details, and tax rules are set up under the Settings navigation heading within the Dashboard. Here you also set your currency details (for international stores, Volusion allows you to function in more than one currency) and you set the exchange rate. You also need to specify your payment gateway, and choose to offer any other payment options to your customers such as PayPal Express, wire transfer, check by mail, etc.

MANAGING YOUR VOLUSION WEBSTORE

Manage your orders, customers, and inventory from these areas of the admin area. Manage marketing from the marketing drop-down, which includes the built-in newsletter system, selling on eBay and Amazon, search engine optimization, social media, Facebook store, affiliate program, etc.

TIP

Bookmark your store and your admin area
Because your development store will have a complicated web address, it makes sense to bookmark both the live site and the admin area so that you can find them again easily. If you need to log in again and haven't bookmarked the addresses, go to www.volusion.com and log in (top right), then from your "My Volusion" screen, click "Manage my store" from the left-hand navigation.

TIP

Connecting a blog to your Volusion store
As with Bigcommerce, there is no in-built blog. If you want to feature a blog, you'll have to set one up externally (on WordPress.com or Blogger) and create a subdomain (e.g. blog.yourdomain.com) that will point to it. For step-by-step instructions, go to: support.volusion.com/article/linking-your-blog-your-volusion-store. When you've created the subdomain, you'll need to create a link to the blog in one of your footer columns—use this code:
<a href="blog.yourdomain.com" target="_blank">Blog</a>

Going live with Volusion

When your store is ready to go live, you'll need to activate it by clicking the orange "Activate My Store" button at the top of the screen. At this point you'll need to decide which package you want to go with, depending on your budget, the features you need, how many products you'll be stocking, and how much bandwidth you estimate you'll need.

Whichever you choose, you'll need to connect a domain name to your store. If you haven't already purchased a domain name, it may make sense to do so through Volusion, so that it is already connected to your webstore. (When you purchase your domain name through Volusion, do so with the same email address that you used to sign up for your webstore, that way the two purchases will be listed under the same account.) If you've already registered your domain name, you need to point the nameservers to Volusion. The required nameservers are ns1.volusion.com, ns2.volusion.com, ns3.volusion.com, and ns4.volusion.com. If your registrar requires just two nameservers, use 3 and 4.

As mentioned, you also need to purchase an SSL (secure sockets layer, see page 33) for your site. This can only be done once your domain is live. Purchase it from the Services > SSL Certificates area of the Volusion home page—they will install it for you.

Getting help with Volusion

Volusion is a complex system, so it's just as well the support is good. There's a Live Chat link on your admin dashboard, as well as a contact telephone number. The Knowledge Base link (under Resources on your dashboard) links to a very thorough article database. There's also a series of video guides accessible from the dashboard (although at the time of writing the links all point to the same place). Volusion also has an e-commerce information section at onlinebusiness.volusion.com, which although it doesn't directly help with Volusion, makes for interesting reading, and a series of webinars here: www.volusion.com/webinar.

8

In focus: WordPress

WORDPRESS IS A LOW-COST ONLINE STORE
SOLUTION THAT ALLOWS YOU TO RETAIN
COMPLETE CONTROL OF YOUR SITE.

An online store with
WORDPRESS AND WOOCOMMERCE

WordPress wasn't conceived as an online store—it began as a blogging tool—but it has developed hugely over the last few years and is now the most used content management system ("CMS") around—that is, a system that allows users to log in and create a website without knowing anything about programming. It features in this book as it is now very often used as an online store as well. But why would you choose it if it wasn't really conceived for this purpose?

The answer is that it is low-cost—you can run it on your website for free, and you're not tied into the monthly charges of a webstore provider. Of course, there will be

the costs of your hosting, and your payment gateway, and you may choose to use a premium theme as well, but these will be significantly lower than if you used an all-in-one webstore. The downside is that you will have to do a bit of technical fiddling around to set it up, and it will require quite a steep learning curve to get going with it, but chances are that if you are on a budget, the benefit may well offset this inconvenience.

Quite another reason why you might favor WordPress is that you get to keep your website entirely in your own hands, and you aren't tied in to a particular webstore provider. It is *your* online business, and in

WooThemes are the makers of WooCommerce, and the creators of a collection of beautiful themes made to work with the plugin. There are also many independently designed themes that go with WooCommerce.

choosing to run it on WordPress, you remain completely in control (as well, of course, as being in charge of security issues, adhering to legal requirements, etc.).

WordPress alone doesn't have the functionality of an online store, so to make it work as one, you have to add a plugin —a piece of code created by an independent third-party that isn't actually a part of WordPress. There are several plugins that can add e-commerce functionality to WordPress, and the one we're going to look at in the walkthough in this chapter is WooCommerce.

There are other excellent e-commerce plugins that can be used, WP e-Commerce and Jigoshop to name just two, however we focus on WooCommerce here, as it's grown massively in popularity recently and has some very attractive themes designed to go with it.

INSTALLING WORDPRESS

Back in Chapter 2, we talked about choosing a web host. You may have chosen to go with one of the hosting companies suggested, and we'll look here at how to install WordPress on both of these, but if you've chosen another, you can simply follow the install directions on their site.

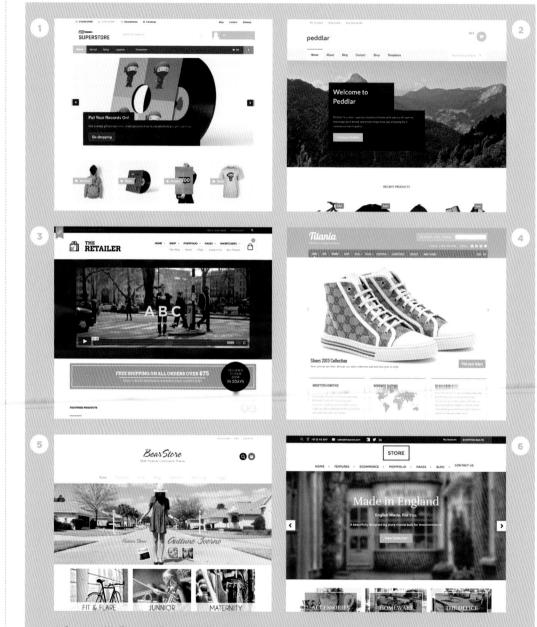

1. Superstore (WooThemes) 2. Peddlar (WooThemes) 3. The Retailer (Getbowtied, available from ThemeForest.net)
4. Titania (UFOThemes, available from ThemeForest.net) 5. BearStore (Novaworks, available from ThemeForest.net) 6. Store (Obox)

Installing WordPress on Dreamhost

1. Log into your control panel. Toward the top of the left-hand navigation, under "Toolbox," click "One-Click Installs." Then click "WordPress" (as shown).

2. In the window that pops up, click the large blue "Custom Installation" button.

3. Select your domain from the drop-down menu and click "Install it for me now!" (Leave the field to the right blank, unless you don't want to install your online store directly onto the main domain.)

4. Check your email, and when it arrives, click the link in the email underneath "1. Please create an admin user at:"

5. In the browser window that opens up, fill in a "Site Title" (this can easily be changed later), a password, and your email address. Uncheck the checkbox next to "Allow search engines to index this site," because you don't want your new store to be accessible before it is ready. Then click "Install WordPress."

6. On the next screen, click "Log in" (and log in)—your setup is complete.

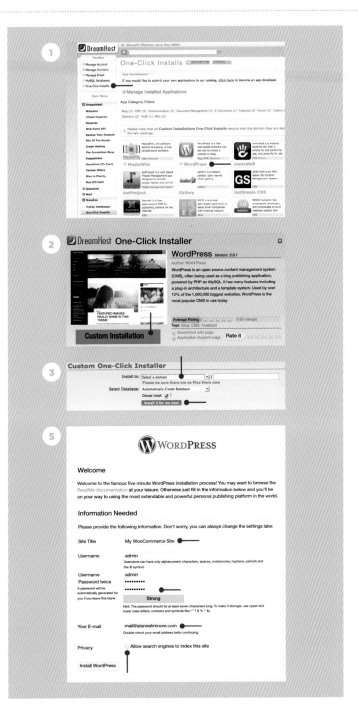

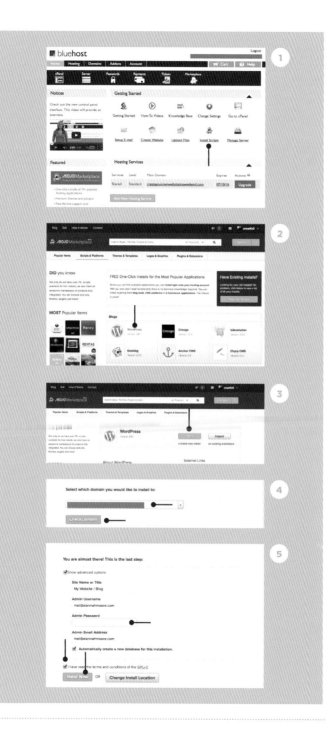

Installing WordPress on Bluehost

1. Log into your Bluehost control panel and click "Install Scripts."

2. Click "WordPress."

3. Click "Start."

4. Choose your domain from the drop-down menu and click "Check Domain."

5. Check the checkbox that says "Show advanced options." Replace the automatically generated password with something you can remember more easily. Check the checkbox next to "I have read the terms and conditions of the GPLv2" and click "Install Now."

6. When you see that the install has completed, scroll down a little bit and underneath "Step 1," click the link next to "Login URL." You can simply log in with your email address and the password you chose. You don't need to bother coming back for Step 2, which suggests that you install a theme, as we'll do all of that from inside the admin area.

INSTALLING WOOCOMMERCE AND THE MYSTILE THEME

For this walkthrough we'll use the free Mystile theme by WooThemes. Note that if you choose a theme from WooThemes, the setup will be very similar, even if the theme is different, but if you choose a theme designed by another theme creator, the installation process for WooCommerce will be the same, but the theme will be customized differently.

1. Go to www.woothemes.com/products/mystile, register for a WooThemes account, and download the free theme. (You will have to pass through a shopping cart process, but the theme is in fact free; once you've "ordered," click the "Downloads" tab and download the theme. You'll also receive an email containing the download link.)

2. The theme may have been unzipped for you by your browser following the download. If that's the case, locate the downloaded folder named ("mystile") on your computer, right-click on it, and select "Compress mystile" to zip the file up again. (If it has remained zipped, you can ignore this step.)

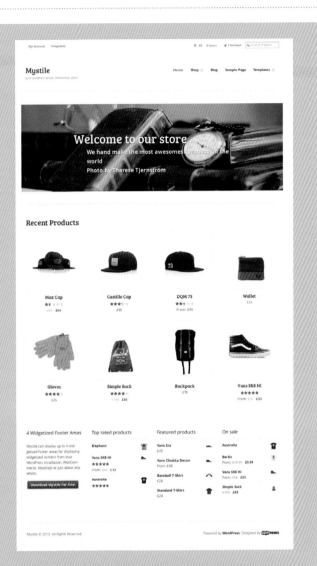

Mystile is a free theme designed by WooThemes to run with WooCommerce. It's highly customizable and therefore suitable for all kinds of online store.

3. From within the WordPress admin area, if you click on the title of your new website from the dark gray strip at the top left (as shown in the screenshot; I named my demo site "My WooCommerce Site"), you can toggle backwards and forwards between the live website and the admin area. If you visit the live site, you can see that the default theme is installed; you now need to upload the Mystile theme to your WordPress installation.

So, from the WordPress Dashboard, navigate to Appearance > Themes, and click the "Add New" button at the top of the screen.

4. Click "Upload," as shown in the screenshot.

5. Click "Browse" and navigate to the "mystile.zip" file. Select it, and click "Open" or "Choose," then "Install Now."

6. When it has installed, click "Activate."

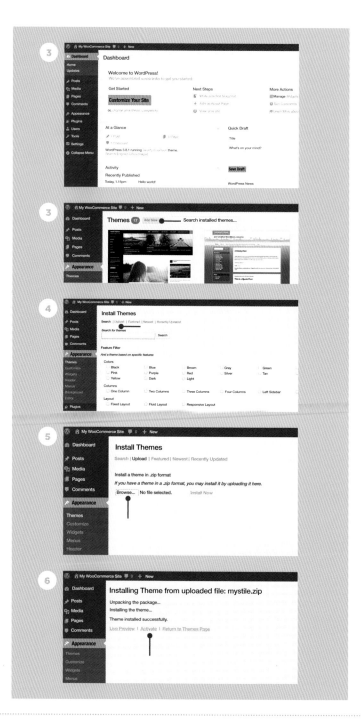

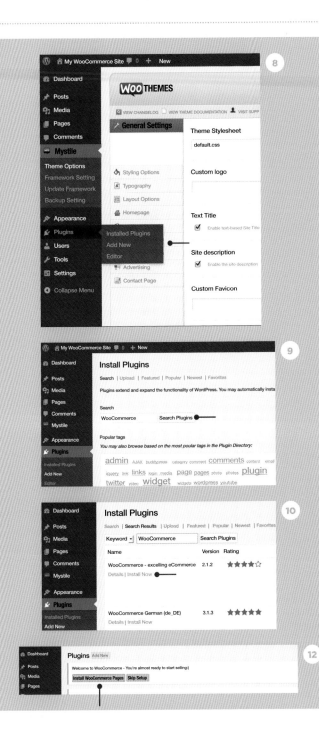

7. Once you've installed your theme, you may see some invitations toward the top of your page asking you to install various extras. You can safely delete these boxes and ignore the invitations as I will guide you through what you need to install.

8. You are now at the main customization area of your theme; however, before beginning the customization, you need to install the WooCommerce plugin. Go to Plugins > Add New from the left-hand navigation.

9. Type "WooCommerce" in the "Search" field and click "Search Plugins."

10. Click "Install Now" beneath "WooCommerce—excelling eCommerce," then "OK."

11. Click "Activate Plugin."

12. Click on the purple button that says "Install WooCommerce Pages."

13. **WooCommerce is now in place, but before you start setting it up, there are a few steps to take.**

i. Go to Settings > General and choose your time zone. You can also change the site title and tagline (subtitle; optional) here as well. Save the change by clicking the blue button.

ii. If you weren't offered the option to tell the search engines not to list your site during the setup process, do it now: go to Settings > Reading and check "Discourage search engines from indexing this site." Save. (You will, of course, change this when your store is ready.)

iii. Go to Settings > Discussion and uncheck "Allow people to post comments on new articles." This is because you won't want people to be able to leave comments at the bottom of your site pages, which you will be setting up in due course. However, since you will probably want people to be able to leave comments on your blog posts (assuming you are planning to incorporate a blog), before creating your blog posts, you

will come back here and switch the comments on again. (This is merely a convenience for you, as you can turn them on and off for each individual page or blog post from within the editing area of each individual page or post.) Save the setting.

iv. Go to Settings > Permalinks and select "Post name." Then scroll a little further down and choose how you'd like your product pages to be named. I suggest "Shop base with category." Click "Save Changes." If you don't make these changes, WordPress will give you clumsy web addresses for your pages, products, and posts (like www.yourdomain.com/?p=1). If you make the changes, your products and pages will have addresses that incorporate your titles, product names, and categories, and therefore will be useful for the search engines.

v. Go to Users > Your Profile and choose how you would like to be named when you post to your blog and reply to comments—"admin" is the default, but it's very unengaging.

CUSTOMIZING THE MYSTILE THEME

We'll now move on and begin a more fun part of the store construction, which is customizing the theme. Click on Mystile > Theme Options. You will see that there are a large number of options available—you'll want to have a good look around, but let's make sure you've seen the important ones.

1. At General Settings > Quick Start, you can change the color scheme of the site and optionally upload a logo.

2. When you click on "Display Options," you can choose to enable "breadcrumbs" on your site. Breadcrumbs are a navigational aid—for example "Furniture > Chairs > Wooden," which let your site visitors see exactly where they are within the store.

3. Under Styling Options > Background, you can choose a background color or image for the store, which is a great way of giving your site instant personality. Note that you must go to the Layout Options tab and check "Enable Boxed Layout" so your background shows up.

4. Go to Styling Options > Links, where you can change your link and button colors.

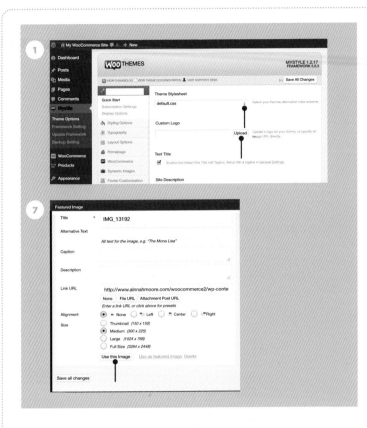

up too much of the home page space. Therefore, resize it to a width of 1120 pixels with a height of about 360, then upload it. Click the "Use this image" button within the window that opens up.

8. The Sidebar, WooCommerce, and Blog tabs, underneath the Featured Image tab, allow you to decide what appears on your home page. You'll need to come back here when you have products in your store. The same applies to the "WooCommerce" section just underneath this, which you'll also need to come back to.

9. The Footer Customization tab allows you to decide how many widgets (individual elements) you'd like across the bottom of the site. These are generally used for lists of bestselling products, featured products, etc.—we'll set these up later. You can also type in your copyright notice and any other information, which will appear left and right at the very bottom of the page.

5. Click on "Typography," if you want to change the fonts of the site. Make sure you tick the checkbox at the top of the screen next to "Enable Custom Typography" to allow your selection to be visible.

6. On the Layout Options screen you can choose to put a border around your site, which will give you the option of using a background image or color. You can also choose whether the store sidebar will be on the left or the right side.

7. Homepage > Featured image is where you decide if you want to have a large banner image on the home page (like the one saying "Welcome to our store" that you can see on the Mystile theme screenshot on page 121). Check the box, and add a heading and subheading. It's probably easiest to resize the image before you upload it using an image editor (or Pixlr.com). The system will resize it to the right width, but you don't want the image to be too high, or it will use

10. The Subscribe & Connect area allows you to put a MailChimp sign-up link at the bottom of every blog post, together with social media badges. (See Chapters 12 and 13.)

11. The Contact tab is where you add your email and physical address, and, optionally, configure a Google Map to appear on your Contact page if you also have a physical store you want to encourage people to come to.

SETTING UP WOOCOMMERCE

WooCommerce has many features that you will want to investigate as they will assist with the running of your business, but here we'll go through the setup as this is more complicated.

1. Go to WooCommerce > Settings (from the main left-hand navigation). Under the General tab, set your country, currency, and the countries to which you are planning to ship goods to. You can also choose whether you want to allow people to make purchases without creating an account.

2. Under the Products tab, set the price display options suitable for your currency, and choose some display options for your products such as size and weight—you may need these for some shipping methods—and whether to allow customers to rate products.

3. Under Inventory (click the link at the top of the screen, underneath the Products tab), you'll probably want to enable the built-in stock management system and allow customers to see stock levels on the site.

4. Set up your taxes under the Tax tab.

5. Go to Pages > Add New from the left-hand navigation and create a "Terms & Conditions" page. (If it's more convenient, you can simply type the title at this stage, and come back and fill in the actual content of the page later.) Save this page, then return to WooCommerce > Settings. Under the Checkout tab, select the page you've just created using the drop-down next to "Terms Page ID."

6. To make your payments PCI-compliant (see chapter 15) you'll need to either purchase, install, and setup a premium extension from WooThemes, or sign up for Mijireh Checkout, which is free to set up and comes bundled with WooCommerce. (That is, unless you are just using the basic PayPal system—PayPal Payments Standard—for which you will not need anything extra).

To set up Mijireh, click "Mijireh Checkout" from the row of links toward the top of

Where to get e-commerce themes for WordPress

As mentioned, there are dozens of beautiful themes available to use with WordPress, whether you're using WooCommerce or another plugin to power your store. Some good places to look for themes are:

> WooThemes (www.woothemes.com)—themes by the makers of WooCommerce
> ThemeForest (themeforest.net)—a marketplace listing thousands of themes created by independent designers
> Creative Market (creativemarket.com/themes/wordpress)—another marketplace showcasing themes by independent designers
> Organic Themes (organicthemes.com)
> ColorLabs (colorlabsproject.com)
> ThemeTrust (themetrust.com)
> Elegant Themes (www.elegantthemes.com)

the Checkout area, then the blue "Join for free" button. (When you've signed up, choose the "DIY" option.)

From the Mijireh dashboard, copy the access key and paste it into the box back in your WordPress admin area, not forgetting to select the checkbox to enable Mijireh Checkout; save the change. Now check your email and confirm your email address by clicking the link in the email you've received from Mijireh. Back at the Mijireh dashboard, configure the settings with your payment processor information and then click the green "Go Live" button at the bottom right of your dashboard.

If you're not using a payment gateway other than PayPal Payments Standard, or you just want to accept payment via cash, transfer, or check,

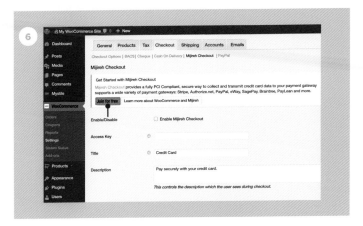

you don't need any extension and you don't need to sign up for Mijireh Checkout. If this is the case, simply use the links across the top of the "Checkout" screen to input the details of the various payment options you're going to implement.

7. Under Shipping, enter details of the shipping methods that you are going to use (using the row of links toward the top of the screen).

8. You don't need to change anything from within the Accounts area, unless you specifically want to. Lastly, the emails the system sends can be optionally customized from within the Emails area.

SETTING UP YOUR PRODUCTS AND COMPLETING YOUR STORE

Now that you've configured WooCommerce, you can start setting up your products.

1. Go to Products > Add Product from the left-hand navigation.

Products are added as follows:

1. Type the product name here.
2. The long description you type here will appear on the page underneath the image under the Description tab.
3. Create categories and assign your products to them.
4. Give tags to your products—these function as keywords.
5. Add extra pictures here.
6. Insert the main product image here and click "Use as featured image" within the window that opens up.

7. Include product details here: SKU (stock keeping unit), price, inventory, shipping, cross-sells and upsells (under Linked Products), and product variations (see the box opposite). Enable product reviews under Advanced, and if you need to send the customer any additional information in the purchase note after buying this product, add it in this area as well.
8. The short description is important as it is the first description that will be seen, appearing under the product title on the product page.

Adding product variations (colors, sizes, etc.)

Select "Variable Product" from the drop-down labeled "Product Data." Under Attributes, click the "Add" button, then name the attribute (for example, "Color"), and add the values, separated by a "|" (e.g. "Blue|Red"). Check the two checkboxes "Visible on the product page" and "Used for variations," and save the product with the "Save attributes" button. Under the Variations tab to the left, choose your default and click "Add Variation." Type the prices and the other details you need to add, and click "Publish" (or "Update") to save the product.

2. Now that you've set up your products, you can decide how you'd like them displayed on your home page. Go back to Mystile > Theme Options > Homepage > WooCommerce and choose how to show your product categories, recent products, and featured products.

3. Your home page is now in place, but you'll need to add other pages on your site. WooCommerce has automatically created the pages you need for your store for you, but you'll need other site pages, such as your "About" page, "Frequently Asked Questions," "Contact," etc., and (optionally) add a blog as well.

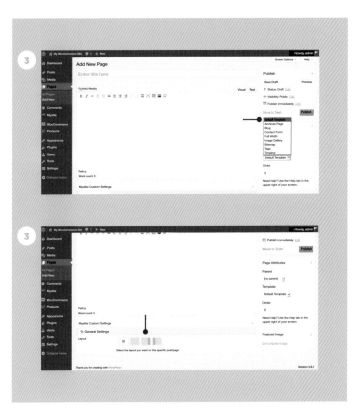

Go to the Pages section of the site and delete the Sample Page that WordPress has created for you. Then click "Add New" to start making your pages, just as you did for the "Terms & Conditions" page. For the blog page and the contact page, you will need to assign the specific layout created by the theme for those pages from within the Page Attributes pane, as shown in the screenshot on page 129. (For an ordinary page, you can keep the setting at the "Default" template.) Note that when you create the blog page, you need to leave the page empty—this page will automatically be filled with your blog posts as you create them later from the Posts area of the admin. Any text you type will not show up, so you should leave the page completely blank. You can choose the layout for individual pages (sidebar on the right, the left, or no sidebar, for example) from within the Mystile Custom Settings pane at the bottom of the page (as also shown on page 129); settings made here will override the general settings within the Theme Options area.

4. You now need to specify which widgets (individual elements) appear in the sidebars of the pages on your site that contain a sidebar, and at the bottom of your pages. Go to the Appearance > Widgets area, where to the right, you'll see some panes labeled "Primary," "Footer 1," "Footer 2," "Footer 3," and "Footer 4." The panes can be opened by clicking on the small triangle to the right of each title. WordPress has put some widgets in for you; you can remove the ones you don't want by dragging them to the left or clicking "Delete." Simply move the ones you want into each pane and configure each one as necessary before clicking "Save."

JETPACK

Jetpack is a collection of additions you can add to a WordPress site, including a Facebook faces widget that you may want to add to your blog. If you want to explore these options, activate Jetpack from within the Plugins > Installed Plugins area. You'll need to sign up for a WordPress.com account to do this, but that's no problem—you don't actually have to use the WordPress.com system, and you'll need to sign up for it anyway to activate Akismet (see step 7). Once Jetpack is activated, you'll see new widgets appearing in your Widgets area that you can then drag into your sidebar or footer.

5. Now you need to set up menus for your store. At this stage the menu on your site will look very messy, with lots of extra e-commerce pages and the pages you've added appearing in the order you created them, but you'll be able to organize them in the way you want. The theme allows you two menus, though you can create additional custom menus and use the Custom Menu widget for your sidebars, if you want to. The main menu goes in the primary position, and you can also create a second menu, which will appear at the very top of the site (ideal for items like Terms & Conditions).

Go to Appearance > Menus and create two menus by clicking the "create a new menu" link toward the top of the screen. You can call them whatever you like, but "Main" and "Top" would be obvious. Then assign them to the correct place in the theme either using the checkboxes (see the screenshot) or within the Manage Locations tab.

Now, in the Pages pane, add pages to your menus by selecting them and clicking "Add to Menu." For the main menu, you don't need to include all the pages that WooCommerce has created for you. For example, the "My Account" page has links to

the pages where users can update their address and make other changes, so there is no need to add the "Edit My Address" or the "Change Password" pages to the menu as well. You will certainly need to add some of these items as drop-downs, otherwise there will not be room for all the items. Do this by indenting the sub-menu items by dragging them slightly to the right with your mouse.

6. If you're going to use the blog feature on your site, you need to add some blog posts so there is some content there when your store launches. As mentioned, blog posts are added within the Posts area of the admin (go to Posts > Add New). If you go to Mystile > Theme Options > Homepage > Blog, you can decide whether you want your blog posts to show up on the home page, and if so, how many posts should be displayed.

7. The penultimate step is to add four plugins to your site. Plugins are extras that aren't actually part of WordPress but you can add them to give extra functionality.

   i. Go to Plugins > Installed Plugins and activate Akismet. This is a very powerful spam blocker, and you'll need it so that you don't get a torrent of comment spam (which you will probably receive, even if you don't have a blog in action on your site). To do this, you'll need to sign up with WordPress. com, if you didn't already do so, to install Jetpack (see the box on page 130). For commercial sites Akismet is paid-for, but believe me, you really will

need it; you can choose how much you want to pay per year.

   ii. You may also want to sign up for Google Analytics in order to track your visitors (see page 137). If you do this, you'll need to add the Google Analytics for WordPress plugin. Go to Plugins > Add New, search for, install, and activate Google Analytics for WordPress. You'll need a Google account to sign up for Google Analytics; when you've done this, add your website address as an "account" within Google Analytics, and copy your tracking ID, which will begin with "UA." The easiest way to set it up is to manually paste in your tracking ID, an option you'll see when you open the plugin settings.

   iii. Add the WordPress SEO by Yoast plugin to help you prepare your store for the search engines (searching, installing, and activating from Plugins > Add New, as above). This will allow you to add titles and descriptions to your pages and your products, and ensure that your content is correctly targeted toward your

desired keywords (more about this in Chapter 11). Don't forget to allow the search engines access to your site once your store is ready! Go to Settings > Reading and deselect the checkbox next to "Discourage search engines from indexing this site."

   iv. Add, and configure, the BackupWordPress plugin in order to automate backups to your site. Because you are running your online store independently, you need to be responsible for your own backups.

8. You'll want to test your store before you go live. The easiest way to do so is by creating a low-cost product and performing the purchase yourself. If you're using PayPal, the site offers a sandbox facility for testing, but it will be more straightforward for you to carry out your own test purchase. When you've done that successfully, your store is ready to go live.

Managing your store

You can view reports, track inventory, create coupons, and manage the status of your orders within the WooCommerce area of the administration. Your customer list can be viewed from the Customers tab within the Reports area.

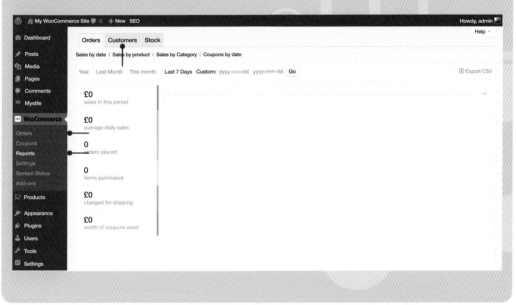

Getting help with WooCommerce

WooCommerce has its own documentation here: docs.woothemes.com/document/woocommerce. The site also has a knowledge base here: support.woothemes.com/forums. Its videos will be useful for those new to WordPress: www.woothemes.com/videos.

9

Running your online store

CREATING YOUR STORE IS JUST THE FIRST STEP; YOUR BUSINESS WILL GROW AND YOU'LL NEED TO HAVE SYSTEMS IN PLACE TO ENSURE IT ALL RUNS SMOOTHLY.

Fulfilling YOUR ORDERS

It's all too easy to forget the customer's perspective when you're creating an online store. You may put so much effort into creating a beautiful, smoothly functioning website that the follow-up somehow assumes secondary importance. However, while it's obvious that purchasing from your site has to be an easy and pleasant experience, for the customer, the emphasis is actually on receiving, and enjoying, the item they have ordered.

You may feel that once the order is completed and the payment on the way to your bank, your part of the work is done—but in fact, the most important part from the customer's point of view is still to come. Today, speed is of the essence in fulfilling orders. Customers won't wait even a week to receive an object—unless, of course, it's extremely special, custom-made, and comes from the other side of the world. People expect fast dispatch, sometimes even the very day the order has been placed. It's crucial, therefore, that you have your fulfillment system well organized.

Most small businesses choose to fulfill their orders themselves when they're starting out. This means a lot of packing, printing of labels, trips to the post office, and liaison with your chosen delivery service, as well as handling all returns and exchanges yourself. This has its positive side—handling order fulfillment yourself saves a lot of money at this crucial time, and you get to interact directly with your clients, which is both useful for working out potential problems and establishing answers to frequently asked questions. It also reinforces a positive image of your brand, as it will be you personally who handles enquiries, deals with problems, and so on.

But when it reaches the point where fulfillment is eating up time that would be better spent creating or sourcing new products, or marketing your store, then it's time to outsource. At the most modest level, this could mean employing a friend part-time to handle dispatch and answer customer service emails (though do remember people expect a fast response these days, certainly within 24 hours). At a more sophisticated level, it might mean outsourcing to a fulfillment house who will handle everything for you, from warehousing, order processing, packing, gift wrapping, and shipping, to dealing with returns and exchanges. You simply pass on the orders to the chosen fulfillment center; in some cases, your webstore platform may offer integration, so the fulfillment center receives and can start acting on orders immediately.

If you use a fulfillment center, your customers will probably end up having more contact with the staff there than with you, so it's essential your chosen company fulfills your ideas of efficient, accurate dispatch and excellent customer service. The impression they give is the impression your customers will have of you. A good way to find out if their service is up to your expectations is to ask for past and current client references and check thoroughly how satisfied the other webstore owners are. Another area to check is if the company has specific experience with the type of goods you're providing, especially if they need any kind of special handling or assembly. If you are going to be shipping internationally, make sure the company is familiar with the necessary procedures.

TIP

Choosing a fulfillment house

Choose a fulfillment house based near your customers rather than near you—you'll save shipping costs that way. Also make sure they can be reached easily if you need to contact them about a change in shipping address for a particular order, or any other urgent matter.

Points to consider when planning the running of your online business:

> Keep the customers informed: notify them when their order has been dispatched, providing tracking information when possible (there are apps for some of the webstore systems that can do this for you).

> Show what's in stock on your website, don't backlog orders—customers will cancel their orders if they have to wait, necessitating a refund and creating bad feeling.

> Keep a steady flow of stock available. If you use a fulfillment service, you should be able to monitor stock levels online.

> You need to be competitive with your pricing as prospective customers will usually compare prices. If you can't afford to cut your prices, offer superior customer service and after sales support to stand out.

> Always remember that customer service is key to a customer's loyalty. It's much easier to get repeat orders from customers who already know you than to find new customers, and it's a lot cheaper in terms of marketing.

DROPSHIPPING

Dropshipping means buying products individually from a wholesaler who ships them to your customers directly as orders come in. You only manage the selling part, cutting out the need to spend large sums on inventory, as well as sidestepping the whole business of delivery and dispatch. There's a useful article on the Shopify site where you can find out more about Dropshipping, as well as a free guide.

INTEGRATING WITH YOUR WEBSTORE SYSTEM

The more sophisticated platforms (including WordPress) offer their users integrations with systems that can automate many of the time-consuming aspects of running your business, or at least, help you cut some corners, even if it is as simple as printing out postage stamps or shipping labels directly from your own printer, thereby saving you loads of time copying and pasting and working out rates. Which third-party integrations you choose depends on where you are based and what your needs are; there are a vast number available—the best advice when choosing a webstore system is to first work out what you will need and then see which can best accommodate these needs.

Some of the integrations available are:

Stamps.com, USPS, Royal Mail, Canada Post, Australia Post, FedEx calculators, OrderCup, Shipstation (streamlining orders and shipping), Ordoro (shipping and inventory management), AfterShip (order tracking and delivery updates), Shipwire, Fulfillrite, Webgistix, Whiplash (fulfillment), Softcookies (QuickBooks), FreshBooks, eBridge Connections (different accounting packages), and Lettuce (all-in-one inventory, shipping and accountancy package, works with Shopify).

Plan before choosing your platform

It pays to think carefully about how your business is going to be run, even before choosing the system you're going to use to create the store. Integrating with a fulfillment center could be crucial to the smooth processing of your orders, especially if you see your business growing fast. It could even mean you don't have to employ anyone else to handle this part of the business. Another huge timesaver will be integrating with an accountancy software such as QuickBooks or Peachtree—if you use these, or plan to down the line, it makes sense to choose a system at the outset which will work with your chosen software.

GOOGLE ANALYTICS

Right from the start, you'll want to track the visitors to your store, to see where they're coming from, at what times, with which search terms, and so on. The best way to track your visitors is by using Google Analytics. To get set up, go to www.google.com/analytics and sign up with your Google login. Add your webstore URL as an "account," copy the tracking code Google provides you with, and paste it into your webstore page template as per the instructions provided by your webstore provider. For WordPress, add it via the Google Analytics for WordPress plugin.

Shipwire (www.shipwire.com) is a large fulfillment center with warehouses in the U.S., UK, Canada, and China, and new ones opening soon in Australia, Germany, and Brazil. You can completely automate your delivery via Shipwire if you're using Shopify, Bigcommerce, Volusion, or WordPress with WooCommerce. To work with smaller fulfillment companies, you will need to forward your orders by email or input orders into an online interface.

Wix, Shopify (shown here), Bigcommerce, Volusion, and WooCommerce all offer a large number of add-ons you can use to add extra functionality to your site and help with the management of your webstore.

10

Marketing

MARKETING IS AN INTEGRAL PART OF YOUR
WEBSTORE CREATION AND WILL BE AN
ONGOING PART OF YOUR ONLINE BUSINESS.

Marketing OPTIONS

You'll need to have marketing in mind
throughout the planning process and the
construction of your online store, and you'll
also need to have a strategy in place for
once the store has gone live.

We've already talked about your USP—your
unique selling point—and how the "look" of
your website, in other words how you brand
yourself, is essential so that you appeal to
your customers in the right way. These are
the first marketing decisions you make for
your online store. So, in fact, are many other

aspects of creating your store. How you
write, for example, reinforces your image;
whether your tone is formal, or lighter and
shows humor.

Once your site is launched, it's your marketing
strategy that will take it from being a brand
new, unvisited store to a busy and successful
store that takes orders around the clock, gets
talked about, generates plenty of glowing
product and customer service reviews, and
brings back repeat customers. So, how can
you market your store?

OFFLINE MARKETING

It's easy to assume that because this is an online store, all your marketing should also happen online. This is a mistake. You'll actually be able to advertise your site far more easily, to more people, more quickly, and often more cheaply, if you market in the real world.

Offline marketing ideas include:

> Being present, or having a stand at shows and fairs. You may even be able to take orders from your online store via a tablet. These are also great opportunities to collect email addresses for your email list—see Chapter 13.
> Direct mailing. You can expect a response rate of about 1% (higher than most forms of online marketing) but it does require a considerable investment upfront.
> Getting articles written about you. This, of course, could be online as well.
> Getting interviewed on the radio.
> Running print adverts in newspapers and magazines.
> Carrying and distributing postcards or fliers that are attractive, clever, or funny, that people may want to send or pin up.
> Encouraging people to recommend you, perhaps with rewards.
> Distributing coupons.
> Including fliers, coupons, and details of promotions in packages you dispatch to encourage repeat orders.
> Always carrying business cards and giving them out at every opportunity.

TIP

Giving a good impression
Every detail of your presentation, your packing slips and invoices, the packaging you send your products out in, conveys an impression. It all contributes to public perception of your brand.

SEARCH ENGINES

In terms of the online world, discovering your online store via the search engines is perhaps the most obvious way of people coming across you. As we mentioned before, when discussing your USP, if your field of interest is a niche topic, you stand a very good chance of getting traffic to your site from the search engines, providing there isn't too much competition. Getting the highest possible ranking for a site has evolved into a complicated pseudo-science known as "SEO" (Search Engine Optimization), and while you probably don't need to become an expert in this, you do need to understand a certain amount about it in order to stand any chance at all of your site appearing in a good position for the relevant keywords. This is so important that we've devoted a whole chapter to the subject—see Chapter 11.

TIP

Create a schedule and stick to it

There's nothing more dispiriting than a blog that isn't updated— it creates the worst impression imaginable. You don't need to blog every week, but do make it regular; if you can't keep your blog up to date, don't have one.

SOCIAL MEDIA

Using social media—Facebook, Twitter, Pinterest, and so on—is a unique way of interacting with your customers and spreading the word about your company and your products. We'll discuss ideas as to how you can make the most of social media in Chapter 12. In order to use social media, you need something to talk about, apart from simply your products, which is where content marketing comes in (see below).

BLOGGING AND OTHER "CONTENT MARKETING" IDEAS

Content marketing is material that relates to your products, or field of interest, that you can put on your website for others to read, refer to, and share. One of the best content marketing strategies that an online store can implement is blogging.

Why would you want to have a blog on your online store?

> It fleshes out the image your customers and potential customers have of you (rather like your About page can, only even more so). It makes you real, and, hopefully, also interesting.
> It engages people in a way that a store can't, even if the store looks beautiful and your wording is fun.
> It establishes you as a leader in your market, the store of choice to come to.
> Whatever your USP is, a blog can reinforce it.
> It makes you very difficult to copy, as the personality and "flavor" of your store will be unique.
> It makes your site look up-to-the-moment.
> It gives people something interesting to tweet or post on Facebook (which they are more likely to do than clicking on the social media links underneath your products).
> It's great for the search engines—blogs contain loads of relevant keywords and will act as "link bait" (meaning other websites will link to it). The search engines also lap up website material that is frequently updated; a major reason in itself to start a blog.

Blogging is time-consuming and will not bring rewards immediately, but after a while of consistent posting, it will start to bring you a steady stream of traffic that is interested in your products.

Blogging ideas:
> announcements, such as new products
> reviews
> comparison of products
> trends
> how-to articles
> interviews with or "spotlights" on the creator or designer of your products
> the story behind certain products
> interesting/successful use of your products, plus photos, as sent in by customers
> customer competitions
> behind the scenes at a product photoshoot
> top tens: "ten ways to…"/ "ten reasons to…" types of articles
> guest posts (where you invite other people to write a post for your blog; or someone invites you to write on theirs

Luxury jeans retailer 3x1 (3x1.us) uses beautiful photography to accompany its blog posts.

15 Mercer —
EVENTS AT 3×1

3×1 is the perfect venue for your next corporate or private event! Based in SoHo NYC, the space boasts 16' lofted ceilings and a bright, spacious atmosphere. The largest collection of selvedge denim in the world is on display along … Continue reading →
11/10/2013

Friends of 3x1 —
PEDRO ANDRADE'S NEW MORNING ROUTINE

We're super proud of our friend Pedro Andrade for the launch of his new program 'The Morning Show' on ABC's Fusion! The show premiered yesterday with a smart, high-energy vibe, not to mention a healthy dose of Pedro's stunning good looks! … Continue reading →
10/30/2013

The Purist —
FALL DENIM

Looking at inspiring blogs created to accompany online stores, such as these ones, will give you plenty of great content ideas. From top left: inkandspindle.com, www.shoon.com, www.bonjourmoncoussin.com.

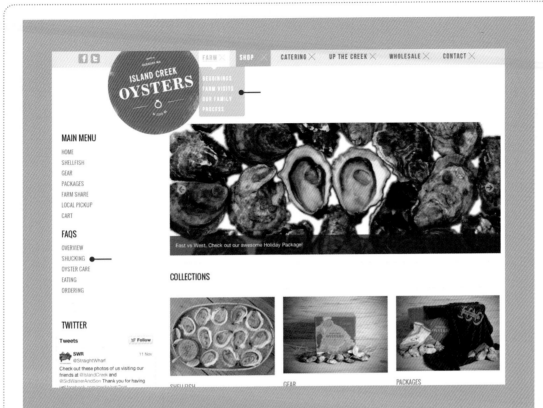

East vs West, Check out our awesome Holiday Package!

COLLECTIONS

SHELLFISH

GEAR

PACKAGES

You can also create extra "meat" for your site in the form of additional site content, rather than (or as well as) a blog. For example, you could flesh out your "About" pages into several, giving your story, details of the people who work for you, and any interesting background; in short creating a "story" for your business. FAQs also provide an ideal source of content you can add to your site. They can be expanded into a series of pages, as you can see with the Island Creek Oysters website above, which includes information on what to eat with your oysters, oyster care, and how to shuck them, and incorporates a demonstration video.

Other ideas for content marketing are posting videos and photos. Product reviews and how-to demonstrations work brilliantly on YouTube. You can then embed them onto a site page, as in the oyster shucking example above. Post photos on Flickr and share them with Pinterest and Instagram (see Chapter 12).

The Island Creek Oysters site develops the story of the business, details the process behind oyster cultivation, and gives oyster care, eating, and shucking tips, so that the site carries much more valuable information than merely selling oysters and the branded accessories that are also on offer. Above: islandcreekoysters.com.

PPC (PAY PER CLICK)

You'll have almost certainly noticed the ads that appear at the top and to the right when you do a search on Google. This is "PPC" (Pay Per Click) advertising, one of the quickest methods of getting traffic to your store, and it it can be extremely effective.

It works like this: the advertiser chooses the keywords for which they want the ad to appear and pays according to the number of "clickthroughs" the advert receives. Be careful as it can quickly get expensive—keywords with heavy competition can cost you. However, you can set your budget per day, to make sure you don't accrue huge bills, and with a little experimentation, you'll settle on a balance between the cost of a click for a certain keyword and the business it generates for you.

As well as being instant, another benefit of this type of advertising is that it is very flexible. You can run ads on certain days for special offers, you can suspend an ad if the specific item is out of stock, or you can change the details if necessary.

PPC ads can be set up on Google (Google Adwords) and Yahoo and Bing (Microsoft Adcenter). You can also run ads on Facebook, LinkedIn, and Amazon (Amazon Product Ads; you don't need an Amazon storefront to participate, as the ads can link to an external website). See also the "Google Shopping and Comparison Shopping Engines" box in Chapter 14, page 164.

Google ads are visible at the top and to the right of a Google search listing; the pictures you can see are images of products listed with Google Shopping, and the stars are from online reviews. See pages 164–165.

AFFILIATE PROGRAMS

Running an affiliate program is a great way of getting others to sell your products for you. It works like this: you allow other people to recommend your products, and if someone purchases on their recommendation, they get a percentage as a reward. Sales are logged and percentages are calculated automatically. For example, if you sell craft products and the owner of a craft blog writes an article mentioning your products, he or she can include a special link to your store, and from within your system, you'd be able to see if a buyer had come directly from their recommendation and made a purchase. You then pay the reward monthly, quarterly, or however often you agree. Some webstore systems offer you a built-in affiliate marketing system, and for others there are affiliate program apps you can add.

PARTNERSHIPS

A partnership isn't quite the same thing but it's along the same lines. You simply strike up an agreement with someone in a different field from you, but who has customers with a similar profile. You refer your customers to them, and they refer their customers to you. This could be in the way of a recommendation in a newsletter, which they then reciprocate, or the inclusion of a promotional flyer or a coupon in all packages shipped, and so on.

Of course, you have to be careful in choosing the companies with which you partner. You have to be sure they reflect your values and that they offer the same high levels of customer service that you do.

CUSTOMER SERVICE

As we have mentioned, customer service is key. If someone enjoys dealing with you, they'll not only speak well about you to others, but they'll also be more disposed to coming back for more. It's so much easier to cultivate a relationship with someone who has already agreed to buy your products, than try to convert a new site visitor into a paying customer. So, treasure your customers, and make sure your after-sales service is superlative. We'll look into some of the ways you can encourage your customers to come back for more in Chapter 14.

TIP

If you have a brick-and-mortar point of sale, you'll want to get a listing on Google Places (www.google.com/local/business/add) and Yahoo Local (smallbusiness.yahoo.com/local-listings/basic-listing).

11

The search engines

GETTING YOUR STORE AND YOUR PRODUCTS FOUND IN THE SEARCH ENGINES IS KEY TO THE SUCCESS OF YOUR ONLINE BUSINESS. IF PEOPLE CAN'T FIND YOUR SITE, THEY CAN'T BUY YOUR PRODUCTS.

SEO BASICS

As we've mentioned, Search Engine Optimization (SEO)—which means, in brief, doing what you can to ensure that your website is as visible as it can possibly be in the search engines—has evolved into a complex "science." This chapter covers the basics of what you need to know.

If SEO is a major consideration for you, in that you need to compete in the search engine rankings with competitors selling similar products to make or break your online business, it will be an ongoing process requiring serious analysis and planning, and you may need to do more specialized reading to equip yourself with the necessary knowledge.

There are a few common misconceptions concerning SEO that we should do away with right away. Firstly, there isn't any trickery that can help you prepare your online store for the search engines. In order to rank websites, the search engines use a sorting method (called an algorithm) that changes frequently to make absolutely certain the search engine is listing sites as accurately as possible. It's simply your job as a webstore owner to prepare your store so that the search engines can list it in the right place. There is no longer the possibility (though this was common practice back at the beginning of the web) of "stuffing" your site with relevant keywords, or packing them into the coding of your site to hoodwink the search engines.

Secondly, you can't buy a good position in the search engines. You can, of course, buy ads on Google, but appearing in what's called a "natural" search—that is, appearing in the listing, hopefully in a high-up position, when someone types a relevant keyword—is purely a matter of how the search engines have analyzed your subject matter, and how "important" they understand your store to be.

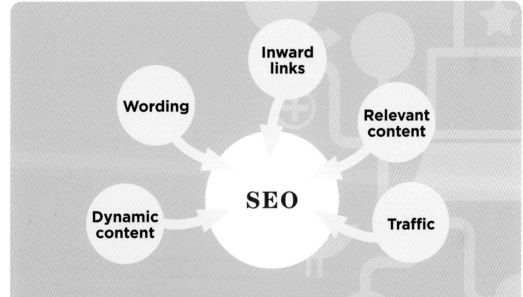

The following factors will influence how the search engines read your site.

1. The wording you have included on your site. The search engines read the text of your website and analyze its subject matter.
2. How often your site is updated. The search engines love dynamic, up-to-the-moment content.
3. The size of your site. If it's a tiny site, it will sink below the larger ones in the rankings.

(Extra website content has got to be relevant, however.)

4. How much traffic you get. A popular site will rise in the rankings.
5. How many other sites link to you. This shows popularity—it's another measure of how "important" a site is perceived to be by the search engines. (The sites that link to you should be relevant to your subject matter.)

WHAT YOU CAN DO TO PREPARE YOUR ONLINE STORE FOR THE SEARCH ENGINES

Before you do anything, work out which keywords and phrases you are going to concentrate on (see the box). You'll need keywords and phrases for your home page, and for each of your products.

1. Pay careful attention to your keywords and phrases when composing the text for the pages of your online store and for your individual products. Headings are especially important to the search engines, particularly the largest ones (labeled as "<h1>" in website code). Make sure you repeat your keywords in your text without sounding strange—apart from alienating your customers, you could also find yourself penalized for artificially including obvious repetitions.

2. There are three key areas within the code of your website that you need to pay attention to. Webstore platforms usually let you set these for each individual page of the site and for each product without going into the code. (If you're using WordPress, you can use a plugin such as WordPress SEO by Yoast or All in One SEO Pack to input these.)

KEYWORDS AND PHRASES

SEO is all about keywords. Your keywords are the words you expect people to be typing into Google if they are looking for products like yours (key phrases are simply clusters of words). In order to prepare your site for the search engines, you need to be very clear on your most important keywords and phrases, and those that you also want to include but that can be classed as of secondary importance. For example, "pet products" and "pet supplies" might be your major key phrases, with "dog treats" and "dog chews" among your secondary.

Ties Mens Ties Dicount Neckties Silk Neckties Men Silk...
www.kohls.com/
Provider of Handmade Silk Necties, Discount Neckties, Mens Silk Ties, Cufflinks, Affordable Ties and Bowties.
Bow Ties - Tie Bars - Neck Ties - Skiny Ties

Shop Ties & Mens Ties - Macy's
www1.macys.com/shop/mens-clothing/ties?id=53239
Browse our slection of Ties an Mens ties. Free shipping with any $99 Ties purchase now at Macys.

Ties & Pocket Squares for Men Nordstom
shop.nordstrom.com/men/accessories
Free shipping on men's ties at Nordstrom.com. Shop neckties, bow ties & pocket Squares from the best brands of ties fo men. Totally free shipping & retuns.

Men's Ties - Accessories Kohls
www.kohls.com/.../shop/mens-ties-accessories.jsp?CN=4294723349...
Enjoy free shipping and easy returns every day at Kohl's. Find great deal on Mens Ties at Kohl's today.

Men's Ties Neckties £ Bow Ties in Colors & Patterns JoS.A. Bank
www.josbank.com/menswear/shop/ties
Look your best in polka dot or paisley pattern tie this spring and summer, Find ties perfect for work or weddings that offer the refined look you love. Or, choose a...

Men's Ties, Formal Silk Ties, Striped and Plain Ties Slaters
www.slaters.co.uk > Suits $ Tailoring > Shirts & Ties
An extensive range of stylish and affordable ties that will make any suit look great! Range includes branded and Slater own brand Ties. Shop online at...

Page titles and descriptions as shown in Google.com for a search for "men's ties." Notice how the page titles show the keywords first, followed by the brand or store name, and that the descriptions have been crafted to sound engaging to the reader, to encourage them to click and visit the website.

i. The page titles (see the screenshot left)

This is the title that shows up at the top of your browser window when you are surfing the web. This is important for the search engines, and is the title that will show up in the rankings. Your most important keywords should be in here, but keep it short—any more than 65 characters won't show up. If you include your brand or store name, put it at the end after your main keywords, separated by a "|" or a "-". Make sure that the keywords you put into your page titles are also present in the actual page text.

ii. The page descriptions (see the screenshot left)

This is the description you can see under the title in the search engines. This text should include your keywords, but here you're also writing for the real, human user. If your description is appealing, it's much more likely the person reading it will click through to visit your site. Don't go over 165 characters.

Most webstore platforms allow you to add titles, descriptions, and keywords for each page on the site (and with some systems, for each product), as well as specifying the web address of each page. Here we can see the Shopify (top) and Wix (above) interfaces for the home pages and the interior pages of the store. Shopify doesn't include a keywords field, as these are widely regarded as redundant when entered into the code of a website. Note that Shopify allows you to add titles and descriptions for each product whereas this isn't possible with Wix at present.

iii. Keywords

Putting keywords into the code of your online store is less important than it used to be, as search engines probably don't refer to these any more (though of course, putting your keywords into the actual text of your site is absolutely essential). However, if you have the option to do this, you might as well put in the keywords and phrases you chose for each page, separated by a comma.

3. Pay attention to your page names or URLs. Your system may allow you to name the web addresses of your pages; if it does, name your pages in a way that is meaningful for the search engines.

4. Name your images in a useful way. While the search engines can't "see" an image, they can read its filename. Instead of simply adding your images to your site with their existing filenames—for example "DEA_3022.jpg"—rename them with a meaningful filename, such as "metal-table-lamp.jpg."

5. It's likely that when you upload images you'll be offered the chance to provide an "alt" (alternative) tag. These no longer serve their original purpose—which was to allow internet users with slow dial-up connections to switch off images and instead read what the images should be on the web pages they were viewing—but they do provide the search engines with information as to the content of the image, so you should be sure to use this opportunity.

6. Create an XML sitemap ("sitemap.xml") for your store. This is a sitemap that the users don't see, but it helps the search engine crawlers ("bots") access all the pages of your site and see how often they are updated. Most systems allow you to generate a sitemap or will create one automatically for you. If using WordPress, you can use the Google XML Sitemaps plugin.

ONGOING TACTICS TO IMPROVE YOUR SEARCH ENGINE VISIBILITY

1. Work on getting links to your site from other websites. Getting online coverage of your store is one way of doing this.

2. Consider blogging and developing other content alongside your store, as the increase in relevant material will increase your "weight" in the eyes of the search engines, and as we've already stressed, they love material that's updated often.

3. Promote your site in other ways, including offline marketing (see page 139), as the increase in traffic will boost your ranking.

TIP

A Yahoo Directory listing?
This is a costly investment ($299 a year) that is probably not worth the expense for a small business, since Yahoo is no longer the search engine market leader. But if you have a real-world base for your store, you can get a free listing in Yahoo Local, as with Google Places (see the tip on page 145).

Submitting your site to the search engines

Google is by far the most important search engine, with Yahoo and Bing holding smaller slices of the pie—while they appear to be separate search engines, Yahoo listings are actually powered by Bing, so you don't need to submit to them separately. Baidu has its own, smaller segment, but it's for Chinese-language users; Yandex, similarly, dominates the Russian market. It's very likely that your site will be found by the major search engines very rapidly without you having to do anything, but you can submit your site manually if you don't find your site automatically listed.

To submit to Google

(you'll need to have a Google Webmaster Tools account):
www.google.com/webmasters/tools/submit-url

To submit to Bing (and Yahoo):
www.bing.com/toolbox/submit-site-url

To submit to Baidu:
zhanzhang.baidu.com/sitesubmit/index

To submit to Yandex:
webmaster.yandex.com/addurl.xml

TIP

Be realistic with your search engine ambitions
If you're a small business and your products aren't super-niche (which would mean you'd be easily found in a search), it may be best to focus on other marketing techniques. If you're not on page one for your major keywords, it's unlikely you'll get a lot of traffic this way.

Webmaster tools

Both Google and Bing offer a suite of "Webmaster Tools" that will help you make sure your store is prepared effectively for the search engines. Sign up for each and submit your sitemap URL. Once signed up, you'll be able to check that the search engines can read all the pages of your site correctly, and you can see how your store is listed in the rankings for your different keywords and phrases.

Google Webmaster Tools

(sign in with a Google account):
www.google.com/webmasters

Bing Webmaster Tools

(sign in with a Microsoft account):
www.bing.com/toolbox/webmaster

Registering your store with Google and Bing Webmaster Tools allows you to check it's in good health for the search engines, and see what search terms it's being found under.

12

Social media

SOCIAL MEDIA IS OF ENORMOUS IMPORTANCE TO BUSINESSES, ESPECIALLY THOSE THAT FUNCTION ONLINE. YOUR POTENTIAL CUSTOMERS ARE HANGING OUT THERE AND YOUR COMPETITORS ARE USING IT, SO TUNING IN TO PROMOTE YOUR NEW ONLINE STORE IS A NO-BRAINER.

Social media OPTIONS

Most online store sytems give you a whole range of tools to help you connect your store and your chosen networks.

At the time of writing, using Facebook and Twitter is standard practice for online businesses. Pinterest has also become a powerful selling tool; YouTube is the world's second-largest search engine; and smartphone app Instagram has developed into a popular way of showing off the visual side of your business and reinforcing your brand.

The goal of your social media activity is engagement with your existing and prospective customers, so that they will become loyal fans and buy from you, not just once, but repeatedly. There are dozens of other less-used networks also in existence, and the landscape will change over the next months and years with still more new networks arriving on the scene; what's important is that you are where your customers are.

Social media buttons on your online store

There are three kinds of social media buttons you can use, and you'll most likely want to make use of all of them, if your system allows you to. They are:

1. Badges that link the site visitor to your profile page so they can view what you have posted (and hopefully participate).

2. Buttons that allow visitors to "follow" or "like" you directly from your store, without having to leave it.

3. Buttons that allow visitors to "share" your material (product, blog post, or other content) directly to their network by whichever social media they choose to use.

Connecting your social media to your store will be more limited if you're selling via a storefront, but you don't have to limit your independent social media activity.

Social media content ideas:

> new arrivals

> seasonal ideas

> contests

> special deals—time-sensitive ones are particularly effective

> pictures of people enjoying your products

> requests for opinions and feedback

> most common Q&As

> incentives to get people to interact—a prize for the first, the weirdest, the funniest story/ photo/comment etc.

Pictures of people enjoying your products make great social media material, like these photos sent in by happy customers. Right: www.facebook.com/ the.crabplace.

USING FACEBOOK

> You need a Facebook business page rather than a personal profile to promote your online business. Go to www.facebook.com/pages/create and choose a suitable category from the drop-down in the Brand or Product box to the right. Think carefully when you're choosing your page name, as you'll only be able to change it once.

> The "cover image" is 851 x 315 pixels. It's a good idea to prepare an image to this size beforehand to make sure it displays as you want. The profile picture displays at 160 x 160 pixels, but it needs to be uploaded at a minimum of 180 x 180 pixels.

> Many webstores have a built-in system that lets you display your products as a store within your Facebook page (Wix, Shopify, Volusion; multiple apps also exist that you can add to do this). Some of these allow you to oblige a visitor to "like" you before they can see the store (a practice known as "like-gating"), others allow you to create discounts only accessible once a visitor "likes" the page.

> Images get better results on Facebook than any other kind of post—consider incorporating text into your images so they don't need any extra explanation. If you have a special deal or contest running, consider creating a graphic to promote it. Another idea is instead of simply posting single product images, to do something creative with them, such as putting together collages or photographing your products in groups.

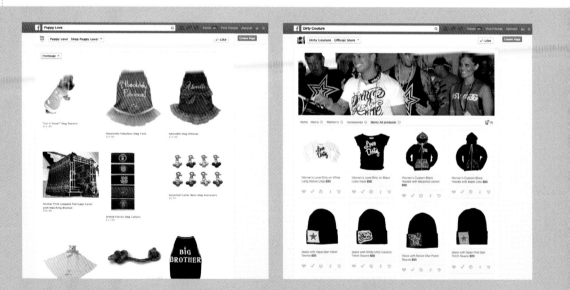

The owners of Puppylove Dogstore (left) use the Fliptabify app with their Shopify store to show their products on their Facebook page. When a user clicks the product, they are automatically transferred to the main webstore. By contrast, the Beetailer Facebook app for Shopify used by Dirty Couture (right), allows the user to add to the cart without leaving Facebook, only going to the webstore to complete their payment. This app also adds other social media buttons to the Facebook store.

USING TWITTER

> Your Twitter profile image (it can be your logo rather than a face) will be displayed at 73 x 73 pixels. It will show up much smaller in the timeline, so make sure the image you upload is clear.

> You need to keep your posts within 140 characters so they need to be both succinct and interesting. Craft your messages with as much care as a newspaper crafts its headlines.

> You can include pictures and videos with your tweets, but users have to click an extra button to see them, so make the accompanying tweet enticing.

> Reply as quickly as you can to customer service questions —even more quickly to any complaints that may arise— to keep down the number of people who see them before you've solved the problem.

> Make use of hashtags in your tweets, e.g. #handmade. This makes it much more likely your tweet will be read by more people.

USING YOUTUBE

> Take the time to customize your channel and write a description of your business. Include tags, allow people to leave comments (you probably want to choose the "with approval" setting), and add your webstore address under the Advanced Options tab so that it shows up on your channel page.

> Don't forget to include your webstore address in the video itself.

> Include your videos within your online store or on your blog.

Ideas for videos:
> testimonials from real customers—great for your website
> how-tos—as well as providing good content that will serve as a marketing tool, online information such as assembly instructions, if relevant, will also boost customer satisfaction
> product demos—much more effective than simple images
> customers using products
> your products being made (perhaps a virtual tour of your workshop?), or any other interesting story behind them

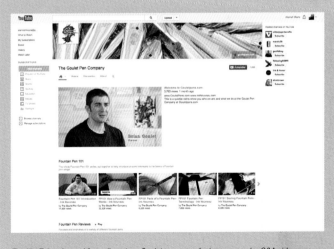

The YouTube channel for online store Gouletpens.com features a regular Q&A video answering real questions asked by customers.

USING PINTEREST

> Pinterest can be an important selling tool—clicks to websites from Pinterest reportedly bring twice as much revenue as those that originate from Facebook.

> To promote your products online, you need a business Pinterest account, so go here: business.pinterest.com (or convert an existing board by clicking the "Convert here" link). You'll need to "verify" your website—this can be done by adding a snippet of code into your webstore template. Ask your webstore's customer support to provide assistance or instructions, if needed. If using WordPress, you can use the Pinterest Verify Plugin.

> Profile images need to be scaled to 160 × 165 pixels. Include a description when you set up your profile as this will help people come across your boards when they search.

> As well as showing your products, Pinterest can be used as a "lookbook" or mood board for your brand. Use your boards to collect all kinds of visual inspiration and flesh out your fans' view of your image.

> Collaborate with others whose products you like—pin their products as well as your own and you'll find yours repinned all over Pinterest as well.

> As per the Facebook tip, create graphics you can pin to advertise your deals.

> When you upload your product images, include a link in the description to the page on your webstore, plus a price, to show the item is for sale.

> Pinterest has recently introduced a feature called "rich pins," which allows product information—price, plus any price change, and whether the product is in stock or not—to appear on a board when someone pins the product image (plus, they also get notified by email when the price changes). If you use Shopify, you can implement this feature relatively easily by following the instructions; just search the Shopify manual for "rich pins." As yet this feature isn't available for other webstore systems, at least not without enlisting the help of a programmer.

> Pinterest also supports videos—these can be pinned from YouTube or Vimeo and will play within Pinterest.

> Ideas for boards other than simply posting your products, or groupings of your products, are: repurposing images from your blog posts; a current deals board (showing graphics of your deals); the people behind the products; and other visual influences.

USING INSTAGRAM

> Featuring images snapped with a mobile phone (Apple or Android), to which filters are optionally applied, has taken off hugely as a way of showing your products in a more creative way.

> You can use Instagram to promote special deals and sales (as in the screenshot shown), or just enjoy creating a more artistic image of your products and your company.

> Sign up via the App Store or Google Play.

Above: modernfurniturecollection.com.

USING GOOGLE+

> At the time of writing, Google+ doesn't have nearly as many users as Facebook but it looks as though it could well become huge. It also has a very nice, clean interface and displays your images, videos, and posts beautifully.

> Google Hangouts—similar to live Skype sessions—are a great way to interact with your customers and they get saved as YouTube videos, so they can be accessed after the scheduled Hangout has passed.

> You need a business page to promote your store, rather than a personal page. Go to www.google.com/+/business and pick a category from the Product or Brand drop-down. Customize your page, post images, videos, and other content just as you would for your Facebook page, and invite your customers to follow you; try to cultivate as much activity on your Google+ page as you can.

13

Email marketing

EMAIL MARKETING IS ONE OF THE MOST EFFECTIVE WAYS TO REMIND PEOPLE ABOUT YOUR PRODUCTS AND ENCOURAGE THEM TO BUY, OR BUY AGAIN.

Promoting your products
BY EMAIL

In order to promote your products via email, you need a list of people to contact. You can't email people without their permission, as this is against the law, nor is it a good idea to purchase a list of email addresses, even if this list is composed of people who have accepted to receive emails from "third parties"—as you usually won't get a good response from people who don't know you. The most effective way of getting results from email marketing is—as with social media—by interacting with people who do know you, whether they've signed up from your website to receive updates or newsletters, or purchased from you in the past. This is called "permission marketing" and it can be really successful because you're attempting to sell to people who you know are already interested in your products.

To manage the list of interested people, you need an account with a third-party email list manager, or ESP (email service provider), unless the system you're using has a built-in list manager, such as Volusion, or if you're running an eBay storefront, which has its own built-in system. Two of the most used third-party email marketing systems are

MailChimp and Constant Contact, although there are dozens of other excellent ones (such as AWeber, iContact, and Mad Mimi). MailChimp is particularly popular as it's free for up to 2,000 subscribers, has an extensive feature list, and many beautiful newsletter templates.

MailChimp is a hugely popular email list manager with a stunning collection of templates you can use. Left: mailchimp.com.

TIP

Connecting your webstore to your email list
In most cases you'll find that an app exists to put a signup form for your mailing list on your site, so visitors can choose to receive your newsletters; if you don't find an app, it'll usually be possible to add an HTML signup form provided by your email list manager.

If it's possible, you'll also want to integrate your customer list with your email list, so that when someone makes a purchase they are added to your email list automatically (otherwise you'll have to do this manually). Most systems offer integrations, but if there isn't an app to connect the two, try doing so via Zapier (zapier.com); you'll need a premium account, but you may find it's worth the cost to save your time.

Stay within the law

There are strict rules governing how you send out your newsletters and follow-up customer emails. Your ESP will help you to a certain extent in that it will automatically include your business address and an unsubscribe link at the bottom of your emails, as required; for more precise information on what you need to do to adhere to the rules, see Chapter 15.

USING EMAIL MARKETING

> Create interesting subject lines—your first goal is to succeed in getting the email opened!

> Who is the email "from"? Sometimes it's more effective to have the email appear as though it's coming from a particular person in the team, rather than simply from the company. It will depend on how you're presenting your company—small and personal or more corporate?

> ESPs usually let you personalize the subject line and/or the email with the receiver's first name. This only works if you're sure you have the right information—not everyone fills in the Name field correctly when they sign up for updates. Another issue is whether it could seem overly familiar to be on first-name terms with your customers— it's your decision.

TIP

Customize your webstore emails

Customize the emails your system sends out: choose your own wording and add your logo (maybe even your social media links) to put your unique stamp on the whole experience.

The Journal Shop.
the world's best stati

Dear Alannah Moore,

Thanks for joining up at The Journal Sh
some of the world's best stationery as
obsessive-compulsive about these thin

Anyway, first things first: let's show yo
Account at the top of every page, and t

Use the following values when pro
E-mail:
Password:

When you log in to your account, you

– Whizz through checkout faster
– Check current orders
– View previous orders
– Change your account information

"Dear Alannah Moore,
Thanks for joining up at The Journal Shop. That was pretty smart of you— now you'll have access to some of the world's best stationery as well as some of the world's best customer service. We're kind of obsessive-compulsive about these things.

Anyway, first things first: let's show you the ropes. To log in…"

Putting a friendly message in an automated email is much more engaging than using boring standard text, so change your automated messages whenever possible. Above: www.thejournalshop.com.

> Once your email has been opened, your goal is to encourage the reader to click over to your store (and hopefully make a purchase). So, make as much as possible in the email "clickable"—your images, product titles, parts of the text, and so on.

> Remember to keep the copy customer-centric. Your text will be much more effective if you focus on benefits, not features, as we talked about in Chapter 5 (see the Christmas newsletter to the right for a great example).

> Include information that doesn't simply promote your products, for example, interesting stories that might feature your products. As well as selling, you are also aiming at building a relationship with your customers, so you don't want to come across too overtly commercial.

> Create a schedule for your mailings. You don't have to send them too often, just make sure they're regular.

> Include a "View in browser" link at the top of your email in case your readers' email software can't read HTML.

"We think that the festive season is a brilliant reason to get crafting, especially to get the kids involved! Why not make your own baubles and decorations? Stockings? Cards? Something for the table maybe? Or how about something just to keep the little elves occupied?"

"This fantastic craft collection is perfect for keeping the kids occupied this festive season!"

This newsletter from a children's craft supplier gives plenty of project ideas as well as promoting its products. Also note the text, which is cleverly written to create the image of busy, occupied creative children in the reader's mind (benefits), rather than simply listing the products and their prices (features). Above: www.littlecraftybugs.co.uk.

> Your ESP will give you the option of creating a text version as well as an HTML version, so opt to do both.

> According to a recent study, email marketing is most effective when the emails are sent on the weekend, and in the evenings between 8pm and midnight.

TIP

Growing your email list
If you exhibit at shows or fairs, collect email addresses for your newsletter, either on a paper form that people can fill in, using a tablet (directly into your mailing list system), or by asking them to leave business cards in a box.

You could also run a competition at a real-world event with one of your products as the prize, and have everyone who enters agree to be added to your email list.

14

Increasing your sales

YOU CAN INCREASE YOUR TRAFFIC THROUGH MARKETING, SEARCH ENGINE OPTIMIZATION, AND SOCIAL MEDIA, BUT YOUR MAIN GOAL WILL BE TO INCREASE YOUR SALES.

Website "CONVERSION"

Now that you have visitors to your site, how do you convert those visitors into buyers?

If you have a hundred visitors to your site a day, and two of these make purchases, that means you have a 2% "conversion rate." You might assume that if you manage to get more visitors to your site, you will achieve more sales, but if you have to pay for advertising to achieve this extra traffic, your profits won't increase at the same rate. It's therefore worth doing everything you

can to increase your conversion rate—that is, turning as many of your existing site visitors as possible into customers.

Website conversion rates vary dramatically according to the field you're in and factors such as how well you're known. They can range from 0.5% up to 10%, or even higher (sites like Amazon.com have conversion rates above 20%). As a general rule, if your conversion rate is 2% or under, there will be ways you can improve it.

Paying attention to the following can have a significant impact on your conversion rate.

> We saw in Chapter 4 how conveying the right image is essential. Does your site look professional? Does your logo strike the right note?

> Do your photographs look professional enough? Do they show your products from all angles, and in enough detail, and in all the different colors available, etc.?

> People want to do business with people they like. We've looked at conveying an image of the company and the people behind it via an "About" page, and how a blog can help to engage your visitors. Does your site interest and engage your prospective customers?

> We discussed the trust factor back in Chapter 5. Does your site reassure your visitors? Do you display payment gateway badges, do you show when products are out of stock, do you clearly show your terms and delivery charges?

> Are your products or services good quality? Will your customers be happy when they receive them?

> Is the price right? As we've said, it's easy for people to compare prices so your prices need to be competitive.

> Can people see reviews on your site? If you can't add independent reviews, you can at least publish ones you've asked for on your site. Do you display any testimonials (e.g. thanking you for your great customer service) prominently, or are they hidden away?

> As we've said, tablets and smartphones are growing in importance with more and more shoppers using them to make online purchases. If your system offers you the option of a mobile version of your webstore (quite often a different design specifically created for mobile use), make sure you enable it from your admin area so that your customers can shop as easily as possible, even via a very small screen. Other systems—such as Wix—will automatically optimize your online store for mobile viewing.

> Make it easy for your customers to buy, and to receive—offer multiple payment options and multiple delivery options.

> Help your customers find what they want. Organize your products into categories, make it easy to search your store, and display the most popular products upfront.

> Can your customers contact you easily? Display a contact number (there are numerous systems offering local or free numbers you can use to forward calls to your own landline or cellphone) as well as an email form for questions, and an online chat facility if appropriate. As we've mentioned, customers expect you to reply to queries fast.

> Do you have an FAQ page on your site? Your goal should be to remove any doubts from the mind of the buyer that might dissuade him or her from following through.

> Do you offer any incentives? For example, time-sensitive special offers, free bonuses, free shipping, if viable.

> Finally, make your site stand out. As we know— you probably do it yourself— consumers carry out research before buying and will most likely visit numerous sites. Do what you can to make them remember yours and come back to make their purchase.

Other ideas to INCREASE YOUR SALES

TURNING CUSTOMERS INTO REPEAT CUSTOMERS

We've looked at many ideas that can help you turn the visitors who come to your website into paying customers. Another way you can increase your sales is by doing everything you possibly can to turn your customers into repeat customers.

We've stressed customer service throughout the book as an essential tool for the small business. It's well known that it makes good business sense for you to cherish your existing customers because it's much easier, and costs you much less, than going out and finding new ones. If you provide a great customer experience (including prompt delivery and excellent product quality) the chances are they'll come back to you, and speak well about you to their friends.

Some ideas to help you secure repeat customers:

> Follow up on sales with a personal email asking for any feedback.
> Keep in touch with your customers (via social media and email).
> Make your customers feel special, part of a club, so they'll feel loyal to you.
> Include extra goodies with deliveries, if possible.
> Include handwritten notes, if possible.
> Offer customer-only promotions.
> Respond personally to good reviews, thanking the customer.
> Respond to complaints by apologizing and rectifying the situation as best and as rapidly as possible—you may well succeed in turning the situation around.

GOOGLE SHOPPING AND COMPARISON SHOPPING ENGINES

The images of products that appear in Google when you conduct a product search (as per the screenshot on page 144) are paid-for ads (PLAs—product listing ads). To have your products appear here, you'll need both a Google Merchant Center Account and a Google Adwords account; go to www.google.com/ads/shopping, link the two accounts together, and set up your data feed as per the instructions. You can also submit your products for inclusion in various comparison shopping engines (CSEs), such as PriceGrabber, Shopzilla, and Shopping.com. These are paid-for services and you'll need to set up separate accounts for each. Apps exist that you can use from within your webstore platform to add your products to the various CSEs and to Google Shopping.

The images of products shown when you search for an item in Google are paid-for ads. To have your products appear in Google's search results, go to www.google.com/ads/shopping, configure your account, and set up a data feed.

ONLINE REVIEWS AND SELLER RATINGS

Online reviews are a powerful way of generating more sales. For seller ratings to show up in Google (whether in the natural search results, AdWords, or Google Shopping listings—see the screenshot on page 144), your customers need to have reviewed your products on a third-party review site such as Trustpilot, PriceGrabber, ResellerRatings, or Epinions; you need at least 30 reviews before Google will show the rating. Alternatively, there are review apps you can add to your store, such as Yotpo, which automatically sends the customer an email asking for a review, once the order has been fulfilled.

Trustpilot is one of several sites that allow customers to leave independent reviews. When you have enough reviews, the number of stars will start showing up in Google next to your listing.

MORE IDEAS TO INCREASE YOUR SALES

> Cross-selling—offering a choice of similar products gives the visitor another chance to buy, if the first product they looked at wasn't exactly what they wanted.
> Upselling—offering an add-on, an accessory, or a more expensive item than the one currently being purchased. Many systems allow you the possibility of offering cross-sells and upsells to your customers.
> Distribute promotion codes.
> Offer gift certificates.
> Offer seasonal promotions.
> Set up a wish list system.
> Create a loyalty program.
> Offer "fans-only" discounts to your social media followers (as we talked about in Chapter 12).
> Offer discounts to newsletter subscribers.
> Listen to your customers to improve the shopping experience. Follow up sales and put a prominent feedback page on your website that encourages customers to comment on their experience. This will not only generate you some nice testimonials, but also allow you to...
> Act on any complaints you receive. People are happy to tell you if they've had a bad shopping experience; turn lemons to lemonade and take action.
> Ask your customers what they want. Perhaps there is something else you could provide that they'd be happy to buy from you?

TIP

Browse around well-known online stores and see what they are doing that you could implement to encourage your visitors to buy.

15

Legalities

WHEN YOU'RE SETTING UP AN E-COMMERCE BUSINESS, THERE ARE A NUMBER OF RULES YOU HAVE TO ADHERE TO.

Considerations

PCI COMPLIANCE

The Payment Card Industry Data Security Standard (PCI DSS) is a set of requirements designed to ensure that all companies that process, store, or transmit credit card information maintain a secure environment. Since you're selling online, you need to make sure your online store complies with these rules. Failing to do so could result in severe penalties, but the good news is that if you're running an eBay or an Amazon storefront, or are using Wix, Shopify, Bigcommerce, or Volusion as a webstore platform, your online store is automatically PCI-compliant. If you're using WordPress, you need to make sure your payment system functions within the guidelines. In the WordPress example in

this book, we signed up with the low-cost Mijireh Checkout service (free to sign up), which works with WooCommerce to make it PCI-compliant.

For more information about PCI-compliance, see these links:

www.pcicomplianceguide.org
www.pcisecuritystandards.org/security_standards/index.php

PRIVACY

Specific laws, depending on which country or state you are based in, demand that you publish a privacy policy on your website. Broadly speaking, this statement declares to your site visitors what information you are gathering from them and what you plan to do with it. Generally, you need to state that you will protect any personal information, such as names and email addresses, and any other consumer information.

See the links below as a starting point, but do check what applies to you according to where you're based.
www.sba.gov/content/privacy-law
www.sba.gov/community/blogs/7-considerations-crafting-online-privacy-policy

COOKIES

Since May 2011, an EU-wide law declares that all websites that use cookies need to display information about the cookies they use and allow the user to opt in or opt out. Cookies are small files stored on a user's computer that web pages can access to determine what is shown on the web page being looked at; these are often regarded as a way of "spying" on consumers, but mostly they simply improve your user experience in simple ways such as showing information on a page the first time you visit it, and not on subsequent visits, or setting the currency on a webstore to the one used where you are.

Since cookies are an essential part of a webstore, if you are based in the EU or you do business with customers in the EU, this applies to you. It isn't as complicated as it may sound to comply with the rules. Some webstore systems will provide a pop-up system that allows users to opt in or out of cookie use on your website with a simple mechanism that allows them to agree to continue browsing. If yours doesn't, you can publish a simple statement announcing that you use cookies and that continued browsing of the site assumes acceptance, and link to a page giving more details of the cookies used. At the time of writing, you'll find Bigcommerce and Shopify have a cookie law solution in place that you can use, plus detailed instructions on how to implement it. WordPress has a large number of easy-to-use plugins you can install. For Wix and Volusion, you'll need to rely on a statement as at the time of writing they don't have a ready-to-use solution.

See this link for more information about the EU Cookie Law:
www.ico.org.uk/for_organisations/%20privacy_and_electronic_communications/%20the_guide/cookies

TRADEMARKS AND COPYRIGHT

You get the rights to your trade name the moment you start using it, but you only get the right to prevent other people from using it when you register it as a trademark.

Trademarks are covered by trademark law and are specific words, symbols, or slogans that identify your products or services. Registering a trademark is important to protect your identity; if you're not protected, you could find someone stealing your identity and your customers once you've built up your business by using your words and slogans. Just as important for a small business is being sure that you aren't unknowingly using someone

PLAYING BY THE RULES
Since rules vary considerably according to where you're based, you're advised to check out the ruling specific to where you are. This chapter will give you a heads-up as to what you need to look into.

else's trademarked words or slogans, as this could mean trouble for you. Trademark research is therefore essential before you start your business; you can pay a specialist firm to carry out the research for you.

Copyright, as distinct from a trademark, is the right of the creator to own creative works such as art, software, or writing. (Note that you can't copyright ideas, but you can copyright their implementation—the artwork, or the words you use to convey them.) When you create a work, it is automatically copyrighted. This means that as soon as your logo appears on a web page, the copyright is yours. You don't have to display a copyright symbol on your website, but if you do, you ᵃⁿⁿᵒᵘⁿᶜᵉ your copyright authority more officially. A usual copyright statement is: "© [YEAR] [Your name]. All rights reserved."

In order to protect yourself further you can officially register your copyright. You may well want to consider this as it's usually relatively inexpensive and uncomplicated, and it will mean your case carries much more weight should you ever need to go to court over copyright issues.

Every country has its own procedures for registering trademarks and copyright. If you're in the U.S., the following links may be useful. www.copyright.gov (United States Copyright Office) www.internetlegal.com/trademark-law-and-the-internetcopyright-law-and-the-internet (Trademark and copyright law and the internet) www.uspto.gov/trademarks/index.jsp (U.S. Patent and Trademark Office)

TAX AND FISCAL RESPONSIBILITIES

Each country, and each state within the U.S., has different rules, so you'll need to research or seek professional advice on what kind of business entity you need to set up, what records you need to keep, and what kind of sales taxes you need to charge your customers.

If you're based in the U.S., the U.S. Small Business Administration website is a good place to get legal and tax information: www.sba.gov

EMAIL

We've mentioned the rules you need to adhere to when you're sending out commercial email. They are not hard to follow:
> Don't add people to your email list without their permission, but you are allowed to add past customers to your list.
> Your message needs to show a correct email address and show the name of the person or business who sent the email.
> You may not use a misleading subject line (you wouldn't want to do this anyway).
> You need to make it clear if the message is an advert rather than an update.
> You need to include your physical business address.
> You need to tell people how to unsubscribe from your list within the email.
> You need to unsubscribe people if they request it (your mailing list manager will take care of this automatically).

For precise information about the requirements of the CAN-SPAM Act, see the link: www.business.ftc.gov/documents/bus61-can-spam-act-compliance-guide-business (CAN-SPAM Compliance Guide)

BUSINESS PERMITS AND OTHER LEGAL REQUIREMENTS

Again, depending on where you are based, you may find you need a permit to do business from your home.

If you're doing business with other countries, you'll need to make sure you comply with international trade laws. See here: www.hg.org/trade.html

If you're based in the U.S., you can apply for a registered trademark online at www.uspto.gov.

If you use a hosted webstore platform like those we look at in this book, or if you sell via an Amazon or an eBay storefront, your online store is automatically PCI-compliant.

Resources

Storefronts/marketplaces
eBay stores.ebay.com
Amazon www.amazon.com
(click "Sell")
Etsy www.etsy.com
Storenvy www.storenvy.com
Bonanza www.bonanza.com
Folksy folksy.com
Bottica boticca.com
ArtFire www.artfire.com
Zibbet www.zibbet.com
Dawanda dawanda.com
Shop Handmade
www.shophandmade.com
Not On The High Street
www.notonthehighstreet.com
The Bazaar bza.co
Zazzle www.zazzle.com
Cafe Press www.cafepress.com
Society 6 society6.com
Luulla www.luulla.com
Made It Myself
www.madeitmyself.com
Craft is Art www.craftisart.com
Craft Cafe www.craftcafe.co
The Craft Star www.thecraftstar.com
Spreadshirt www.spreadshirt.com
Ruby Lane www.rubylane.com
Lilter lilter.com
The Internet Antique Shop
www.tias.com
Go Antiques www.goantiques.com
eBid ebid.net
Webstore www.webstore.com
OLA www.onlineauction.com
Silk Fair www.silkfair.com
eCRATER www.ecrater.com
Addoway www.addoway.com

Hosted webstores
Wix www.wix.com
Shopify www.shopify.com
Bigcommerce
www.bigcommerce.com
Volusion www.volusion.com
Big Cartel bigcartel.com
Squarespace www.squarespace.com
Weebly www.weebly.com
Webs www.webs.com
Jimdo www.jimdo.com
Moonfruit www.moonfruit.com
Create www.create.net

WordPress
Self-hosted WordPress
wordpress.org

WordPress e-commerce plugins
WooCommerce www.woothemes.
com/woocommerce
WP e-Commerce getshopped.org
Jigoshop jigoshop.com
Cart 66 cart66.com

WordPress themes
Themeforest
themeforest.net/category/wordpress
Woothemes www.woothemes.com
Creative Market creativemarket.
com/themes/wordpress/
Organic Themes
www.organicthemes.com
Elegant Themes
www.elegantthemes.com
Theme Trust themetrust.com
Mojo Themes
www.mojo-themes.com
Tokokoo tokokoo.com
ColorLabs colorlabsproject.com
WP Explorer www.wpexplorer.com

Domain name registrars
www.godaddy.com
www.namecheap.com
www.gandi.net
www.101domain.com
www.marcaria.com
betterwhois.com
(find out who owns a domain name)

Choosing a domain name
www.dotomator.com
namestation.com
www.nameboy.com
www.domainsbot.com
www.randomainer.com
impossibility.org
domai.nr

Recommended web hosts
www.bluehost.com
www.dreamhost.com

Payment processors
PayPal www.paypal.com
Authorize.net www.authorize.net
SagePay www.sagepay.co.uk
PSIGate www.psigate.com
WorldPay www.worldpay.com
Stripe stripe.com
Realex www.realexpayments.com

Logo design
Crowd Spring
www.crowdspring.com
Design Crowd
www.designcrowd.com
99 Designs 99designs.com

Fonts
1001 Free Fonts
www.1001freefonts.com

Image editing software
Pixlr pixlr.com
Gimp www.gimp.org
Photoshop Elements
www.adobe.com/uk/products/
photoshop-elements.html

Printing- cards, silk boxes, etc,
Moo moo.com

Tracking
Google Analytics
www.google.com/analytics

Fulfillment
Shipwire shipwire.com

Places to advertise
Google Adwords
adwords.google.com
Bing Ads bingads.microsoft.com
Amazon Product Ads
services.amazon.com/content/
product-ads-on-amazon.htm
Facebook Ads www.facebook.com/
ads/create
LinkedIn Ads www.linkedin.com/ads
Google Shopping
www.google.com/ads/shopping
Google Merchant Center
www.google.com/merchants

Glossary

Get listed in the real world
Google Places www.google.com/local/business/add
Yahoo Local smallbusiness.yahoo.com/local-listings/basic-listing

Search engine submission
Google www.google.com/webmasters/tools/submit-url
Bing/Yahoo www.bing.com/toolbox/submit-site-url
Baidu zhanzhang.baidu.com/sitesubmit/index
Yandex webmaster.yandex.com/addurl.xml

Webmaster tools
Google Webmaster Tools
www.google.com/webmasters
Bing Webmaster Tools
www.bing.com/toolbox/webmaster

Social media
Facebook www.facebook.com
Twitter twitter.com
YouTube www.youtube.com
Pinterest www.pinterest.com
Google+
www.google.com/+/business
Instagram instagram.com

Email marketing
MailChimp mailchimp.com
AWeber www.aweber.com
Constant Contact
www.constantcontact.com
Mad Mimi madmimi.com
iContact www.icontact.com

Automation
Zapier zapier.com

Reviews, price comparison
PriceGrabber
www.pricegrabber.com
Shopzilla www.shopzilla.com
Shopping.com www.shopping.com
Trustpilot www.trustpilot.com
ResellerRatings
www.resellerratings.com
Epinions www.epinions.com
Yotpo www.yotpo.com

Admin area Also known as the "back office" or "back end." This is the part of your website that the public can't see, where you log into and make changes that will show up on the "live" part of the website (also known as the "front end").

Affiliate program A system by which individuals can market other people's products and earn a percentage of the sales price.

Algorithm The method Google and other search engines use to determine the order in which sites are ranked.

App An add-on (sometimes paid-for) created by a third party that you can add to your online store system to make it perform extra functions, for example a loyalty program, product upsells, or a Facebook store.

Blog An area of your site where you post articles, images, videos, and any other material to add extra interest to your online store and provide news updates to the readers.

Browser The software you use to surf the internet (e.g. Chrome, Firefox, Internet Explorer, Safari).

Carousel See Slider.

CDN (Content Distribution Network) A global system of servers used to ensure a webstore runs as quickly and efficiently as possible; most hosted webstore systems use one.

Cookie A small piece of data sent from a website and stored in site visitors' browsers to remember pieces of information such as their geographical location, the currency they use, and what's in their shopping cart.

CRM (Customer Relationship Management) Software used to organize and streamline customer information, sales, marketing, and support. A well known example is Salesforce. Volusion has a built-in CRM system.

CSE (Comparison Shopping Engine) A website that compares the prices of products as available from different online stores.

Domain name A website address, e.g. www.youronlinestore.com.

Dropshipper A wholesale company that ships directly to the customers. The store owner manages the sales and passes the orders to the dropshipper.

Email mailing list A system for emailing your customers or other interested parties who have signed up to receive newsletters or updates from you.

Email marketing The practice of using an email list to keep in touch with your customers (usually with the purpose of encouraging them to purchase again, or persuading potential customers to buy).

ESP (Email Service Provider) The company that maintains your email list; you'll mail out to your list via its online interface.

Extension The end part of a website address, e.g. ".com" or ".co.uk." See TLD.

Favicon A small image, most often a logo, 16x16 pixels in size, that shows next to a website address in the browser address bar, bookmarks list, and in browsing history. Most systems allow you to upload a .png or a .jpg, but if you need to create a .ico file, just do a google search for "ico generator."

Follow To show interest in a company or a store via certain social media so that you can be kept up to date with their news.

Footer The area at the bottom of a web page, which often contains a copyright notice, links to Terms & Conditions, Privacy, etc.

Front end The "live" part of your website that is visible to the public. *See* Admin area.

FTP (File Transfer Protocol) The process of uploading to a website. If you need to add something to your online store outside your admin area, you'll need special software such as CuteFTP (PC) or Fetch (Mac). Your host will provide the FTP login and password.

Fulfillment center/fulfillment house A company that handles the dispatch of your products for you once they've been ordered.

Host/hosting company *See* web host.

Hosted webstore An all-in-one system that runs on the provider's host, meaning you don't have to sign up for a hosting package via a third party.

HTML (Hypertext Markup Language) The basic programming language used to build websites. You won't need to know any to use any of the systems in this book (with the exception of Volusion, which requires you to copy, paste, and adjust already written snippets of code).

Integration Connecting your webstore with third-party systems, often via an app, so that certain tasks happen automatically. For example, subscribers signing up to your MailChimp mailing list directly from your website, shipping rates being calculated, and orders being passed to your fulfillment house.

Internet merchant account A bank account into which you can deposit the sums taken from online sales.

Keyword/key phrase The words for which you anticipate your online store being found, when people conduct a search with Google or any other search engine.

Like To give approval to a company by clicking the Facebook "thumbs up" button on its profile page (or on its website); this will be reported on your Facebook timeline and may also appear on your news feed.

Marketplace A shopping environment online in which the products of many individual vendors are sold. Examples are eBay, Amazon, Etsy, Bottica (and many more).

Menu The navigation area on your website; your site visitors will click the pages on the menu that they want to visit.

Merchant account *See* Internet merchant account.

Navigation *See* Menu.

Payment gateway A service that authorizes credit card payments and sends the payment to your internet merchant account.

PCI-compliance If you take payment over the internet, you need to make sure you adhere to a set of rules concerning cardholder privacy and security as set down by the Payment Card Industry Security Council (see Chapter 15).

Piggyback If you sell via a site such as Amazon, eBay, or Etsy, you benefit from the large amount of website traffic that already visits that site, so you could be considered to be "piggybacking" on the success of that site. *See* Marketplace.

PLA (Product Listing Ad) Adverts on the Google Shopping network that show pictures of your products, alongside their prices, appearing in a Google search.

Platform The framework or system you use for your online store, e.g. Shopify or WordPress.

Plugin An "extra" that you add to your online store system to make it do something that it didn't automatically do "out of the box."

PPC (Pay Per Click) A system of advertising for which you pay each time a user clicks on your ad to visit your online store, for example Google AdWords.

Product feed A file containing a list of your products and their attributes, allowing the content to be included on a price comparison website or as a PLA (product listed with the Google Shopping network).

Registrar The company with which you registered your domain name.

Responsive A website that resizes automatically to display in a legible way when viewed on a smartphone or tablet.

RSS (Rich Site Summary or Really Simple Syndication) Also known as a "feed" or a "web feed," RSS is a way of publishing website content (often blog posts) so it can be read via a feed reader, or published elsewhere. *See also* Product feed.

Search engine When searching for something on the web, you'll use a search engine to find it. By far the most commonly used search engine is Google; other popular search engines include Yahoo! and Bing.

SEO (Search Engine Optimization) The practice of tweaking your site— its content and coding—in order to get the highest possible ranking in the search engines.

Share To mention an article on a website (or a product) to a particular social media network; this is usually done by clicking a Tweet, Pin, or Share on Facebook button directly from the website.

Shopping cart The piece of software that allows your online store customers to select the products they want to buy. It's also where they view the products they've chosen, before moving to the checkout page.

Sidebar The column on the left or on the right of some web pages.

Slider A large image usually toward the top of the home page that displays a sequence of images in rotation. A slider usually contains pictures of seasonal offers or bestsellers, and often has writing in it as well as images to encourage the site visitor to click or buy. This is sometimes known as a "carousel."

Social media Online networks via which users create, share, and exchange information and ideas (e.g. Facebook, Twitter, Pinterest, etc.).

Spam Unrequested email messages, usually containing advertisements. (Also known as Unsolicited Commercial Email—"UCE.")

SSL (Secure Sockets Layer) A system used to encrypt sensitive information input via your website, such as your customers' credit card numbers and other personal data.

Storefront This term can mean an online store in general, but in this book we use the term more precisely to describe the collection of your products displayed on a single page within a larger marketplace environment such as eBay or Amazon.

Subscribe To sign up to receive an email newsletter or to follow a blog by email.

Tag A keyword you can add to a product (or a blog post) to enable your site visitors to find the product via your site search.

Theme Another word for a template. The template you apply will determine the layout, the colors, and the fonts; some may be customizable to a greater or lesser extent (Wix, WordPress, Shopify), but this is not always the case. Other webstores (Bigcommerce, Volusion) don't allow you to customize the themes at all without going into the code.

Thumbnail A small, square image, often of a product. When clicked on, the visitor usually gets to see a larger image, plus details of the product.

TLD (Top Level Domain) Examples are ".com" or ".co.uk." *See* Extension.

Tracking Observing and analyzing your website traffic statistics, in order to understand the geographical location of your visitors, the search terms they used to find your site, the pages they visited, how long they stayed on the site, and so on.

Traffic The visitors to your website.

Tweet A message sent via Twitter.

Upload Putting a file on your website, for example an image file, usually via the admin area of your online store.

URL The address of a site or web page, e.g. www.yourwebstore.com

USP (Unique Selling Point) The factor that sets you apart from your competitors, for example your products being the very latest, or your customer service the best.

Visits Refers to people who visit your website (as distinct from "hits," which are simply the number of times a certain item, such as an image, is viewed on your website).

Web host The company who provides you with space on which to construct your website in cyberspace. Most of the webstore systems in this book are "hosted." *See* Hosted webstore.

Website conversion The practice of trying to encourage your webstore visitors to purchase something and become a paying customer, for example, by ensuring any questions they may have are answered clearly on the site.

Webstore An online store. In the real world, this term is used generally to describe anywhere on the web where a purchase can be made, but in this book, we use it more specifically to mean your own store online, as distinct from adding your products to a larger marketplace such as eBay where you have your own "storefront," that displays your products, but over which you have little branding control.

Wholesaler A company that provides products at a low bulk price, that you, as a store owner, will then sell on to your retail customers at a higher price.

Widget An element, most usually found in the sidebar or in the footer area of your website, such as a Facebook Like button with faces, or customer reviews. Widgets are often provided by third parties for display on your online store.

Index

Acknowledgments

Many thanks to my editors at The Ilex Press—Ellie Wilson, Zara Larcombe, and Nick Jones—and to Laura Hodgson, Elizabeth Milovidov, Sarah Cole, and Hugh Abbott for ideas, encouragement, and brainstorming. Thanks too to all the online store owners who allowed me to include screenshots of their sites, and the webstore/storefront providers who answered my questions.